"Salvation Shall Spread Through All the Tribes and Ranks of Mankind":

Jonathan Edwards and World Mission

"Salvation Shall Spread Through All the Tribes and Ranks of Mankind":

Jonathan Edwards and World Mission

Adam G. Cavalier

Volume 2
A Series of Treatises on Jonathan Edwards

JESociety Press

WWW.JESOCIETY.ORG

Paperback Edition October 13, 2021
ISBN 978-1-7379026-0-7
© 2021 Adam G. Cavalier

A publication of JESociety Press
Visit https://www.jesociety.org

All rights reserved. No part of this publication may be reproduced, distributed, or transmitted in any form or by any means, including photocopying, recording, or other electronic or mechanical methods, without the prior written permission of the author/publisher, except in the case of brief quotations embodied in critical reviews and certain other noncommercial uses permitted by copyright law.

For permission requests and inquiries,
Email: info@jesociety.org
Web: www.jesociety.org

A Series of Treatises on Jonathan Edwards

JESociety Press is pleased to announce *A Series of Treatises on Jonathan Edwards*, an all new series given exclusively to the select publication of cutting-edge research related to America's greatest theologian. The series provides authors with a venue for publishing original, concise, authoritative and peer-reviewed manuscripts. The series provides readers with lively, assessable and in-depth treatments of Edwards-specific subject matter. For more information about the series or with questions about JESociety Press, please visit our website at: www.jesociety.org or contact us directly at: info@jesociety.org.

PRAISE FOR THIS VOLUME

In view of the abundance of literature presenting Jonathan Edwards as a "missionary" or a "theologian," it is rare to find a lacuna in this terrain. Nonetheless, this book makes a fresh contribution by insightfully amalgamating these two dimensions—analyzing Edwards as a theologian of world mission. Adam Cavalier's innovative missional emphasis on familiar treatises such as, *The End for Which God Created the World, Original Sin, Freedom of the Will, An Humble Attempt,* and *Religious Affections* makes not only for a fascinating read but an inspiring one as well.

Chris Chun, PhD
Director of Jonathan Edwards Center and
Professor of Church History at Gateway Seminary

This new work by Dr. Cavalier on the missiological vision of Jonathan Edwards, who has been rightly described as "America's Augustine," provides an important monograph on one of the key ways that Edwards' legacy has impacted the church. English Baptists around William Carey were led, for instance, by their reading of Edwards' literary corpus available to them, to launch out into a bold plan of cross-cultural missions. They disagreed with Edwards on a few details, but his passionate interest in the spread of the Gospel to the ends of the earth that gripped him in turn came to inform powerfully their missional thinking. This compact monograph incisively details the scope of Edwards' thought and its contours and is a very welcome addition to the secondary literature of Edwardsiana.

Michael A.G. Haykin, FRHistS
Chair and Professor of Church History and
Director of The Andrew Fuller Center for Baptist Studies
The Southern Baptist Theological Seminary

Even though Edwards lived before the great century of Protestant missions, his theology is filled with missional instincts which sought the spread of the gospel around the world. Missionary and historical theologian Adam Cavalier skillfully draws together the pertinent texts in Edwards's corpus to demonstrate the missional thrust of his theological vision. He does so in such a way that is both faithful to Edwards and motivational to the missionary cause in the twenty first century.

Robert Caldwell, PhD
Professor of Church History
Southwestern Baptist Theological Seminary

To Magan,

my wife, best friend,

and co-laborer in the gospel

Acknowledgements

This work marks the completion of the most eventful period of my life. The course of my program at Southwestern Baptist Theological Seminary has seen two moves across the world and three children born. In the Fall of 2014, my wife and I finished our three-year commitment to an overseas mission organization. We decided to move back to America to begin my studies at the main campus in Fort Worth, TX. At the time, full residency was required for the PhD program. After about a year and a half into my program, the seminary announced the beginning of flexible access. This format allowed me to move back overseas to continue my ministry. While this new initiative was a tremendous blessing, it required me to sometimes wake up in the middle of the night to join the seminar in progress from overseas.

    Needless to say, all these things have been taxing on my family. I could not have managed to get to this point in my academic career without their love and support. While this dissertation bears my name, they deserve equal credit for whatever benefits may come from it. My parents and in-laws have always given encouragement and support. My parents regularly checked in with me in order to find out how this paper has been progressing. The laptop this dissertation was written on is a blessing of generosity my in-laws have shown time and time again. I do not know where I would be without the encouragement and generosity of my wife's grandmother, Dr. Joann Bowers, whom we affectionately know as "Granny Jo." Finally, my wife deserves even more credit than I could ever give to her. She has given so much to see this dream of a Ph.D. be realized. I love her dearly.

    I am grateful for all the faculty at SWBTS. However, there are a few that mention special recognition. Dr. Jeffrey Bingham has inspired me to pursue the highest degree of academic excellence. Dr. Madison Grace has shown an outstanding degree of care and concern for me throughout the course of my program. He has been a mentor for me both professionally and personally. Dr. Robert Caldwell, my supervising professor, has gone above and beyond to help me in my studies. For these men, I am grateful to the Lord.

Finally, I continue to be amazed at the grace of God in my life. As I reach the end of this program, I am persuaded that Nehemiah 8:10 is crucial–not just for every landmark of theological education, but also every moment of life: "The joy of the Lord is your strength." His grace alone has brought me to this point, and his joy has been the strength that has sustained me.

Adam G. Cavalier, Ph.D.
El Paso, TX
Summer 2021

Contents

Acknowledgements i

Introduction 1
    Survey of Existing Scholarship 2
    Edwards's Theology of Mission, Defined and Sketched 8
    Chapter Synopses 11
    A Case Study in Edwards's Theology of Mission 19

Chapter 1 — The Sovereignty of God   23
    The Foundation of a Theology of Mission:
        A Historical-Theological Survey 24
    Concerning the End for Which God Created the World:
        A Missional Reading 35

Chapter 2 — The Universal Depravity of Humankind   43
    The Need for a Theology of Mission:
        A Historical-Theological Survey 45
    Original Sin: A Missional Reading 57

Chapter 3 — The Universal Ability and Inability of Humankind   69
    The Possibility for a Theology of Mission:
        A Historical-Theological Survey 70
    Freedom of the Will: A Missional Reading 83

Chapter 4 — The Verbal Proclamation of the Gospel   95
    The Method of a Theology of Mission:
        A Historical-Theological Survey 96
    An Humble Attempt: A Missional Reading 109

Chapter 5 — The Conversion of the Heart   117

The Nature of a Theology of Mission:
  A Historical-Theological Survey 118
Religious Affections: A Missional Reading 133

Conclusion   141

Bibliography   145

Index   153

Introduction

"Now the kingdom of Christ shall in the most strict and literal sense extend to all nations and the whole earth."[1] Jonathan Edwards's bold assertion envisioned a future in which the gospel of Jesus Christ would progress into non-Christian lands and eventually the glory of God would encompass the entire earth. The gospel will make steady progress out in the world, as the world would "look to Christ and be saved."[2] The *telos* of human history will be God's glorification in the redemption of the world.[3] Just as the waters cover the seas, God will communicate his glory to the nations by the advancement of Christ's kingdom. Edwards wrote, "There shall be no part of the world of mankind but that shall be covered with the knowledge of God."[4] This abiding hope of the advancement of the Christian religion proved to be a major facet of Edwards's theology. This hope has inspired countless pastors, missionaries, and theologians throughout church

---

[1] Jonathan Edwards, *A History of the Work of Redemption,* ed. John F. Wilson, vol. 9 of *The Works of Jonathan Edwards* [*WJE*] (New Haven: Yale University Press, 1989), 473.

[2] Ibid., c.f. Isaiah 45:22 (KJV), "Look unto me, and be ye saved, all the ends of the earth: for I am God, and there is none else." I have used the KJV translation throughout this paper.

[3] Scholars have debated the scope of Edwards's view of salvation. Anri Morimoto claims Edwards had an inclusivist view, which incorporated those who have never heard of Christ. Gerald McDermott takes a slightly nuanced version of this view. Greg Gilbert rejects both of these perspectives, claiming that Edwards held to a traditional Reformed view. See Greg D. Gilbert, "The Nations Will Worship: Jonathan Edwards and the Salvation of the Heathen," *Trinity Journal* hereafter, *TRINJ* 23 (2002): 53. This paper will take up this question in Chapter 3.

[4] Edwards, *A History of the Work of Redemption, WJE* 9:473.

history. McClymond and McDermott note that Edwards's massive influence has led some to call him the "grandfather of modern Protestant missions."[5]

While numerous projects have shed light on related areas, this paper seeks to fill a lacuna in Edwards studies by presenting a historical-theological construction of Jonathan Edwards's theology of world mission. The major weakness of the current research is that most of the studies have not seen Edwards as a theologian of mission. They have merely presented him as a missionary or as a theologian. While these studies are extraordinarily helpful, they have not taken up extensive historical-theological analyses of the theme of world mission within Edwards's wider theology. But what was Edwards's theology of mission? How can it be identified? This dissertation argues that upon a reading of key texts within the Edwardsian corpus, a coherent theology of mission emerges. Later, we propose a five-part approach to discerning the fundamental component to this theology of mission.

Survey of Existing Scholarship

There has been a recent explosion of scholarly and popular literature aimed at drawing out missiological themes within the biblical text. This approach has become a distinct interpretive method that has shed light on key themes of Scripture.[6] The discipline of missiology has just begun to be applied to the biblical text. The intersection of Scripture and mission is currently being established. However, missiology has yet to be adequately applied to the text of theologians throughout the history of the church, especially in theologians earlier than the late eighteenth century. This research follows these few studies which have sought to locate missions within the theology of past biblical interpreters.[7] This section provides a survey of the current state of

---

[5]Michael J. McClymond and Gerald R. McDermott, "Edwards on (and in) Mission," in *The Theology of Jonathan Edwards* (New Haven: Yale University Press, 2012), 565.

[6]David Bosch, George Peters, Michael Goheen, Craig Bartholomew, Christopher J. H. Wright, George R. Hunsberger, and Richard Baukham have been pioneers in this field. Other scholars include N. T. Wright, Michael J. Gorman, Robert Glover, Gustav Warnek, Walter Kaiser, Avery Willis, and others. Their collective efforts have helped scholars see how missions intersects with biblical hermeneutics. In part, their efforts have been aimed at understanding how our interpretation of Scripture can be enhanced when viewed through the lens of mission.

[7]The late Norwegian missiologist Ingemar Öberg sought to prove the claim that Luther was a missions-minded theologian. While Luther never wrote a systematic exposition on the subject, Öberg contends that when one examines Luther's exposition of Scripture, one must necessarily come to the conclusion that Luther was interested in foreign missions, seeing the need for active missionary engagement in worldwide evangelism. Upon a full consideration of Luther's works–especially his biblical exegesis–Öberg's study revealed that Luther was deeply interested

research regarding our current proposal. Much of the current secondary literature provides a precedent and foundation for our work, but in the end it does not accomplish what we set out to do in this dissertation.

Direct Engagement of Edwards and Mission

Many works have directly engaged the subject of Edwards and his relationship with the theme of mission. In what follows, we will divide this subsection of literature according to two broad categories. The first category of materials that can inform our research is that of historical analysis of Edwards's lived experience as a missionary in Stockbridge, Massachusetts (1751–1758).[8] This subset informs our research as we seek to understand Edwards's lived experience as a missionary. These works are interspersed with information from Edwards's personal journals and letters which provide a window into the inner thought life of the theologian. They also give a social context to the theological works themselves. One study details the extent of Edwards's missional engagement, as it was far-reaching into many different areas of life and ministry.[9]

---

in world missions. Furthermore, his research revealed new insights into Luther's theology by highlighting innovative exegetical methods and creative theological formulations. Not only did Öberg confirm Luther as a missions-minded theologian, but more importantly, he shed light on Luther's theology by interpreting his writings from the lens of missiology. Öberg's research has served as a groundbreaking new study for scholars to find new insights by reevaluate Luther's exegesis and theology along such lines; See Ingemar Öberg, *Luther and World Missions: A Historical and Systematic Study*, trans. Dean Apel (St. Louis: Concordia, 2007). To mention but a few additional examples, see Michael A. G. Haykin and C. Jeffrey Robinson Sr., *To the Ends of the Earth: Calvin's Missional Vision and Legacy* (Wheaton, IL: Crossway, 2014); Thorsen Prill, *Luther, Calvin, and the Mission of the Church: The Mission Theology and Practice of the Reformers* (Munich, Germany: GRIN Verlag, 2017).

[8] Although there are many excellent articles and biographies that cover Edwards's life as a missionary in Stockbridge, Rachel Wheeler's work is the most extensive and authoritative research. See Rachel Margaret Wheeler, "Living upon Hope: Mahicans and Missionaries, 1730–1760," Ph.D. diss., Yale University, 1998; George Marsden's biography of Edwards chronicles this period in detail; See George M. Marsden, *Jonathan Edwards: A Life* (New Haven: Yale University Press, 2003); Cynthia Moore's doctoral dissertation surveys many different colonial missionaries to the Native Americans, with special attention to Edwards; Cynthia Marie Moore, "'Rent and Ragged Relation(s)': Puritans, Indians, and the Management of Congregations in New England, 1647–1776," Ph.D. diss., State University of New York at Stony Brook, 1999; Stephen Nichols's chapter is noteworthy as it shows Edwards as an social advocate for Native American interests as well as a missionary intent on saving souls. See Stephen Nichols, "Last of the Mohican Missionaries: Jonathan Edwards at Stockbridge," in *The Legacy of Jonathan Edwards: American Religion and the Evangelical Tradition*, D. G. Hart, Sean Michael Lucas and Stephen J. Nichols, eds. (Grand Rapids: Baker, 2003), 47–63.

[9] Davies presents Edwards as fulfilling many different roles: a missionary theologian, trainer, practitioner, strategist, administrator, and advocate. See Ronald Davies, "Jonathan Edwards

The second category is that of engagement of Edwards as a theologian of mission. This category should be seen as a broad grouping intended to include anything that might directly engage research at the intersection of Edwards's theology and mission. While there are numerous works that could fit under this wide rubric, our goal focuses on the most important works that are relevant to this paper's argument.

To begin, we must single out Ronald Davies's doctoral dissertation.[10] His fifth chapter, "Theological Interrelations," is the closest study within all of the secondary literature that gets close to what this present dissertation seeks to accomplish. It attempts a systematic presentation of Edwards's missiology. It is especially helpful as it proposes a brief framework for Edwards's theology. However, the dissertation struggles to present a comprehensive theology because of its regular departures from that central theme. For example, Davies gets sidetracked into talking too much about things such as Edwards's antecedents and influences while neglecting a constructive presentation of the theology itself.[11]

Jonathan Gibson's article is helpful in that it sets a precedent for reading Edwards's theological treatises for missiological insights.[12] For example, he starts with Edwards's *The End for Which God Created the World*, saying that the work of redemption is the primary means by which God brings glory to himself. Then, he moves to Edwards's treatise *Original Sin*, stressing all of humanity's need for this divine mission. Finally, Gibson analyses Edwards's *A History of the Work of Redemption*, which communicates the means, extent, and purpose of God's redemptive mission. Gibson says that when these various works are taken together, they can be interpreted into a coherent whole, revealing "the prominence of missions" in Edwards's theology.[13] While he makes this assertion, he does not attempt to present that theology of mission in any substantial way.

(1703–1758): Eschatology and Mission," in *A Heart for Mission: Five Pioneer Thinkers* (Fearn, Scotland: Christian Focus, 2002), 79–96.

[10]Ronald Edwin Davies, "Prepare Ye the Way of the Lord: The Missiological Thought and Practice of Jonathan Edwards (1703–1758)" (Ph.D. diss., Fuller Theological Seminary, 1989).

[11]Davies's second chapter proves to be helpful in understanding Edwards as within a stream of missional theologians. However, it does not look at the actual thought of Edwards. At best, the chapter helps one understand "how much Edwards was an innovator and how much a synthesizer he was in this area." Ibid., 32.

[12]Gibson, "Jonathan Edwards: A Missionary?" 380–402.

[13]Ibid., 397.

McClymond and McDermott's chapter in their monumental *The Theology of Jonathan Edwards* presents Edwards's work as a missionary.[14] It does still offer a window into how Edwards viewed the unbeliever. A history of Edwards—the missionary—intermixed with a particular view on his theological anthropology is the main contribution of this work. Similarly, Greg Gilbert's article provides a helpful analysis of Edwards's view of the unbeliever, specifically as it relates to their inclusion in God's redemptive purposes in history.[15]

Mark Rogers's article informs how Edwards's eschatology drove much of his missional theology.[16] Rogers sees Edwards as largely optimistic of the missionary task due to his interpretation of biblical prophecy coinciding with contemporaneous historical events. His work is especially informative in how it views Edwards's accounts of revivals as theological documents, not merely historical reporting on events.

Earl MacCormac's article claims that "[Edwards's] theology provided a basis for a theology of mission."[17] The article adds to the previously mentioned literature in that it draws out Edwards's theology of mission not only from his theological treatises, but also from various sermons. Again, this essay is profitable in claiming Edwards as a theologian of mission, yet it makes no attempt to present that theology.

Anri Morimoto's article is a brief essay that seeks to further Morimoto's controversial claim of nuanced universalism within Edwards.[18] He does this by reference to dispositional ontology. Morimoto claims that mission is simply actualizing the disposition of the unconverted. "The purpose of mission is to help them realize what they actually are."[19] This essay is helpful insofar as it provides one unique perspective on Edwards's theology of mission.

---

[14] Michael J. McClymond and Gerald R. McDermott, "Edwards on (and in) Mission," 549–565.

[15] Gilbert, "The Nations Will Worship: Jonathan Edwards and the Salvation of the Heathen," 53–76.

[16] Mark C. Rogers, "A Missional Eschatology: Jonathan Edwards, Future Prophecy, and the Spread of the Gospel," *Fides et Historia* 41 (2009): 23–46.

[17] Earl R. MacCormac, "Jonathan Edwards and Missions," in *Journal of the Presbyterian Historical Society* 39 (1961), 219.

[18] Anri Morimoto, "Salvation as Fulfillment of Being: The Soteriology of Jonathan Edwards and Its Implications for Christian Mission." *The Princeton Seminary Bulletin* 20 (1999): 13–23.

[19] Ibid., 22.

Gerald McDermott's essay highlights two key aspects of Edwards's theology of mission.[20] First, Edwards believed the church should be on mission. In contrast to other great Reformed minds, Edwards held a prominent place in his theology for mission. Second, Edwards held to a great sense of optimism for the task itself. He fervently expected spiritual revival to take place in and around his immediate surroundings. These two aspects set him apart in his missiology. Rachel Wheeler's essay contributes to how we may interpret Edwards's theological treatises composed during his time in Stockbridge.[21] These two works excellently combine Edwards's lived experience as a missionary with his theology that supported that missionary enterprise.

Indirect Engagement of Edwards and Mission

Some studies have charted how the missionary theology and zeal of Edwards inspired later generations. These include studies on figures such as William Carey, Richard Furman, Andrew Fuller, and John Piper.[22] These also include how Edwards inspired not just individuals, but also to the formation of whole societies and movements.[23] These works touch on how Edwards's theology motivated missionary zeal.

Numerous introductory studies on the aforementioned works of Edwards inform our research. For example, there is a helpful one-volume work that serves to introduce readers to each of these major works.[24] This introduction

---

[20] Gerald R. McDermott, "Missions and Native Americans," in *The Princeton Companion to Jonathan Edwards* (Princeton, NJ: Princeton University Press, 2005), 258–73.

[21] Rachel Wheeler, "Edwards as Missionary," in *The Cambridge Companion to Jonathan Edwards* (New York: Cambridge University Press, 2007), 196–215.

[22] J. Herbert Kane, *A Concise History of the Christian World Mission,* 84–7; Obbie Todd, "The Influence of Jonathan Edwards on the Missiology and Conversionism of Richard Furman," *Jonathan Edwards Studies* 7 (2017): 36–54; Chris Chun, *The Legacy of Jonathan Edwards in the Theology of Andrew Fuller,* Studies in the History of Christian Traditions (Boston: Brill, 2012); Philip. O. Hopkins, "Missions for the Glory of God: An Analysis of the Missionary Theology of John Piper" (Ph.D. diss., Southeastern Baptist Theological Seminary, 2005).

[23] Although Davies mainly concludes that Edwards's impact was most felt in Reformed communities in England, he broadly traces the legacy of Edwards's influence across many different countries and denominations. See Ronald Davies, *Jonathan Edwards and His Influence on the Development of the Missionary Movement from Britain* (Cambridge: Currents in World Christianity Project, 1996); David W. Kling charts the streams of Edwards's revival theology into the Second Great Awakening. See David W. Kling, "Edwards in the Second Great Awakening: The New Divinity Contributions of Edward Dorr Griffin and Asahel Nettleton," in *After Jonathan Edwards: The Courses of New England Theology,* eds. Oliver D. Crisp and Douglas A. Sweeney (New York: Oxford, 2012).

[24] Nathan A. Finn and Jeremy M. Kimble, eds., *A Reader's Guide to the Major Writings of Jonathan Edwards* (Wheaton, IL: Crossway, 2017). This volume will be helpful in bringing out themes

orients the reader to these works, which in turn assist us in exploring new pathways to missional themes.

One of the areas that is of great interest to this dissertation is the recent work on Edwards's hermeneutics, specifically as it incorporates a notion of the history of the work of redemption.[25] These studies have contributed to our understanding of how Edwards's exegesis directly translated into a narrative history of redemption. This theme gives shape and context to our dissertation of how Edwards understood the kingdom of Christ to advance into non-Christian lands. More specifically, Edwards's history of redemption shapes the pattern, method, nature, and *telos* of his theology of mission.

Edwards's soteriology is also an important area of research. Quite obviously, this area is too vast to mine every detail. Therefore, we must single out studies that directly intersect with key missional themes. Most times, these are explicit, such as in Anri Morimoto's article.[26] Yet, other times, Edwards's theology of mission is hidden in essays that have nothing overtly to do with the theme of mission—such as the scope of the atonement.[27]

Another major point of theology that intersects with our research is Edwards's eschatology. Many scholars have researched Edwards's eschatological vision, but few have connected the missional themes implicit in the works. These few mainly focus their attention on how Edwards's narrative accounts have influenced missionary zeal.[28] One scholar argues that Edwards's eschatology provided a comfort to missionaries to persevere in

---

geared towards practical application. Each chapter ends with a section that is intended to show Edwards's work relevant to daily life and theology.

[25] The most recent and excellent examples of this grouping comes from the work of Douglas Sweeney and David Barshinger. See David Barshinger, *Jonathan Edwards and the Psalms: A Redemptive Historical Vision of Scripture* (New York: Oxford, 2014); David Barshinger and Douglas Sweeney, eds. *Jonathan Edwards and Scripture: Biblical Exegesis in British North America* (New York: Oxford, 2018); Douglas A. Sweeney, *Edwards the Exegete: Biblical Interpretation and Anglo-Protestant Culture on the Edge of the Enlightenment* (New York: Oxford University Press, 2015).

[26] Anri Morimoto, "Salvation as Fulfillment of Being: The Soteriology of Jonathan Edwards and Its Implications for Christian Mission," *The Princeton Seminary Bulletin* 20 (1999): 13–23.

[27] For example, Kenneth Morris presents Edwards as a conflicted theologian. On the one hand, Edwards held to the doctrine of limited atonement. On the other hand, he strongly advocated for a revivalism that was not limited to European elites. This tension made for a disjointed theology of conversion. Kenneth R. Morris, "The Puritan Roots of American Universalism," *Scottish Journal of Theology* 44 (1991): 457–87.

[28] James Manor shows how Edwards's narrative accounts inspired missionary activity in Great Britain. More specifically, he connects Edwards's eschatological vision and his doctrine of natural ability (the insistence on one's ability to immediately repent and believe) with a theology of mission. See James Manor, "The Coming of Britain's Age of Empire and Protestant

suffering.²⁹ Another claims that Edwards's optimistic outlook on the end times played a positive role in missionary endeavors.³⁰ And yet another points to Edwards's eschatological hope as directly inspiring missionary action.³¹ These works serve the purpose of showing how Edwards's theology of mission is broad and expansive. Yet, again, the point must be demonstrated, there is no existing study that clearly outlines, articulates, and explains Edwards's theology of mission.

Edwards's Theology of Mission, Defined and Sketched

A Theology of Mission, Defined

A preliminary definition of a "historical-theological analysis of world mission" is helpful at this point.³² While a seemingly endless scholarly discussion on the definition of mission is ongoing, a broad definition will be used in this study. This expansive classification allows for a wide-ranging scope to our study. In short, the following definition will be used: A historical-theological analysis of mission interprets a given historical text with the goal of drawing out themes that feature the advancement of the Christian religion in the world.³³ These themes are presented in an organized and systematic fashion that allows for easy analysis and understanding of the author's theology of mission. For Edwards, this progress of the Christian religion

---

Mission Theology, 1750–1839," *Zeitschrift für Missionswissenschaft und Religionswissenschaft* 61 (1977): 38–54.

²⁹See Ronald Davies, "Jonathan Edwards: Missionary Biographer, Theologian, Strategist, Administrator, Advocate—and Missionary." *International Bulletin of Missionary Research* 21 (1997): 60–66.

³⁰Berg, Johannes Van Den, *Constrained by Jesus' Love: An Inquiry into the Motives of the Missionary Awakening in Great Britain in the Period between 1698–1815* (Kampen, Netherlands: J. H. Kok, 1956), 83, 91–93.

³¹R. Pierce Beaver, "American Missionary Motivation before the Revolution," *Church History* 31 (1962): 216–26.

³²This paper is aware that the term "mission" is in many ways an anachronism. Edwards was obviously unaware of any modern usage of the word and its implications. We must be careful not to apply any theological term back into Edwards in such a way that would alter Edwards's theological, philosophical, or methodological convictions. We must understand him on his own terms. However, the usage of the term and its cognates is appropriate when the substance of world mission is present. Therefore, whenever we encounter Edwards's theology as its correlates to our definition, we will incorporate it into our research.

³³Similar to Öberg's study, we consider what Edwards has to say about reformation within Christendom, yet there are limits to our present study. The primary focus of this research is Edwards's thinking about foreign mission.

had spiritual as well as ethnic, social, and political connotations. Although the primary vehicle for the advancement of the Christian religion was the verbal proclamation of the gospel, there were also other factors at play that informed how Edwards saw this progress. Again, this proposed definition allows for an expansive range of foci to be included in our research.

A Coherent Theology of Mission, Sketched

Again, our purpose is to construct a coherent theology of mission within Edwards's writings. It can be briefly sketched here in five parts. First, Edwards's theology of mission stresses God's sovereignty in the advancement of the kingdom of Christ on earth. God acts out of his own good pleasure and for his own glory. He is not obligated to save. He dispenses his saving grace on whomever he chooses. Moreover, he rules over human history. God shapes and guides human history towards a definite end. This aspect forms the foundation of Edwards's theology of mission. Edwards believed that the plan and purposes of God were not limited to the polite confines of European society. Even the non-Christian tribes are included in this plan of redemption. All people are made in God's image and are created for a definite purpose—-to glorify God and enjoy him forever.

Second, we see a universal view of human depravity. All of humanity is implicated in the guilt of Adam's sin. Adam's sin is imputed to the entire human race. No one is able to contribute to their own salvation in any way. This fact of life is true for everyone—-both the person who was born into Western society and the person born into a non-Christian tribe. This part forms the need for mission. There are people who stand condemned, dead in their sins. Edwards casts this idea in strictly missional terms. By virtue of the fact that the Christian religion is promised to advance in the world, there is need for God and the church to intervene.

Third, Edwards makes a universal distinction between universal ability and inability. All men are capable of choosing God in that there are no outside constraints, naturally or physically preventing him from that choice. However, all men are incapable in that they do not desire to choose God. There is an inward, moral block in their access to God. Left to themselves, they would remain in sin and judgment. Only God can intervene to save men. Yet, the church's witness is the means by which God does choose to save sinners. This part is the possibility of missions. Edwards's doctrine informed his theology of world mission in that it shows the potentiality of conversion. Without a natural ability to accept or reject the gospel, there would be no real prospect of mission because the possibility is removed. In Edwards's view, there would neither be any real guilt, for they would not willfully participate in Adam's sin. This category creates an existential reality, which enables real mission.

Fourth, there is a need for a verbal proclamation of the gospel. The advancement of the Christian religion comes only through the church's proclamation of that saving message. In our study, we will see how the progress of the gospel will necessarily and inevitably come to a point of cross-cultural engagement. This part is the method of Edwards's theology of mission. The proclamation of the gospel is not just limited to promulgation within Christendom. Flowing out of the aforementioned points, Edwards's theology demands that the gospel be verbally preached across cultures.

Fifth, Edwards emphasizes the religion of the heart. Although Edwards's writings do have overtones of the Christian religion making advances through political, economic, or military power, the way progress truly occurs is through an inward heart transformation. These other forces can ignite, catalyze, spur, or facilitate the progress of the Christian religion. However, the only means by which the Christian religion advances is through an internal conversion of the heart. This part is the nature of true mission. A non-Christian culture can not simply adapt different outward practices. Individuals must repent and believe, each experiencing an authentic transformation of the heart. In sum, these are the elements that we will seek to find and analyze when surveying Edwards's works. Our task will be to read key writings of Edwards and evaluate each of these themes in the process.

In outlining Edwards's theology of mission, a brief of statement concerning the order of presentation is appropriate at this point. Beginning with the sovereignty of God and ending with the effect on a person's heart reflects a taxonomy in the theology of Edwards. His Reformed theology resists any attempt to reverse the order. Therefore, the order of this presentation is reflected in Edwards's own theological convictions.

A Strategy of Presentation

We will accomplish our task of understanding Edward's theology of mission by giving a presentation in two steps. The first step will be a thematic analysis of one of our five missional themes. Here, we will present a wide-angle scope of our investigation and survey all of the relevant treatises, sermons, and other works within the entire Edwardsian corpus that expound upon that particular theme. This approach allows us to see the theology of mission across a broad variety of works. The second step will be a literary analysis of a specific text. This approach allows the reader to see Edwards's theology of mission in a particular theological treatise, which fully embodies one of our five themes. In other words, we will choose a text that fully represents that particular theme. So, for example, our first chapter will analyze Edwards's *Dissertation Concerning the End for Which God Created the World*. We will draw out the missional themes, establishing how Edwards conceived of the sovereignty of God as a foundational basis for a theology of mission. Therefore, each main chapter of this dissertation will consist of two parts.

Chapter Synopses

Introduction

The Introduction consists of this present chapter. This chapter provides the foundation and blueprint for what is to follow.

Chapter One

This chapter, entitled "The Sovereignty of God," provides a survey of Edwards's theme of the sovereignty of God. This theme gives the foundation and source for a theology of mission. We will begin with an examination of a wide variety of works, all of which are mined for their relevance to this overarching theme. For one example, Edwards's *A History of a Work of Redemption* charts the narrative of God's saving work in human history. It shows how Edwards's conceived of the divine plan, identifying three epochs in which God uniquely acts to redeem his creation. In this work, Edwards shows the means by which God will bring about the advancement of the Christian religion in the world.[34] God is seen as sovereign over all of human

---

[34] Michael McClymond theorizes that Edwards's unfinished later work by the same title would have been a transitional shift in his theological focus. He points to his private writings as evidence that Edwards's work might have pivoted away from the Anglo-American experience to the work of God in cultures outside Christendom. He adds that if Edwards finished this tome, his theological legacy might be an even greater impetus towards missionary involvement and activity. See Michael McClymond, "A Different Legacy?: The Cultural Turn in Later Notebooks and the Unwritten History of the Work of Redemption," in *Jonathan Edwards at Home and Abroad: Historical Memories, Cultural Movements, Global Horizons,* David W. Kling and Douglas A. Sweeney, eds. (Columbia: University of South Carolina Press, 2003), 16–39; Gerald McDermott also connects Edwards's view of salvation history to missions. See Gerald R. McDermott, "Missions and Native Americans," in *The Princeton Companion to Jonathan Edwards,* ed. Sang Huyn Lee (Princeton: Princeton University Press, 2005), 258–73.

history, and he is bringing all things towards a definite end. That end is explored in detail in part two of this chapter.

In Edwards's *Dissertation Concerning The End for Which God Created the World*, he observed two great "temporal salvations of God's people" in Scripture—the Exodus from Egypt and the return of the exiles in Babylon.[35] He notes that these two events are often depicted in Scripture as great signs that point towards God's salvation of his people in Christ. Edwards's main point is that these temporal actions are done to vindicate God's name. Yet, there is more to Edwards's point upon closer examination. Edwards wants these two temporal acts of divine redemption to be seen as God vindicating his name among the nations. Edwards provides numerous Scripture references to support his assertion that he acts for his own glory because the unbelieving nations have scorned his name.[36] Moreover, Edwards's shows two major aspects of this vindication. God acts in mercy and in judgment. He judges the nations for their pollution in God's name, and he shows mercy on Israel. Thus, judgment and mercy are subordinate ends in vindicating God's name throughout the entire earth. Edwards says that the glory of God is made manifest through "the conversion of the Gentile nations to true religion."[37]

This divine glory is promised to extend to every corner of the globe. Edwards goes on to explain exactly how this will happen. "The manifestation of glory, the emanation or effulgence of brightness, has relation to the eye. Light or brightness is a quality that has relation to the sense of seeing: we see the luminary by its light."[38] God will communicate himself in his glory, and the nations will see it. Beholding the glory of God is the means by which his name is vindicated in the world.

God is concerned with how his people Israel will act in the nations so that his name is glorified. When Edwards repeatedly refers to Old Testament passages and imagery, he emphasizes a transnational communication of God's glory, where God's name is vindicated across geopolitical, religious,

---

[35] Jonathan Edwards, "Dissertation Concerning The End for Which God Created the World" in *Ethical Writings*, ed. Paul Ramsey, vol. 8 of *The Works of Jonathan Edwards* [*WJE*] (New Haven: Yale University Press, 1989), 494.

[36] Nearly every verse cited by Edwards comes from the Old Testament. This strategy is Edwards's way of highlighting the national identity of God's people in relation to the surrounding Gentile people.

[37] Edwards, "Dissertation Concerning The End for Which God Created the World" *WJE* 8:496.

[38] Ibid., 521.

and ethnic lines.[39] Again, Edwards sees God's two temporal acts of deliverance (Exodus and return from Babylon) as a way of displaying divine glory to the unbelieving nations. Because these acts are aimed at displaying God's glory among the nations, it necessarily entails the progress of the Christian religion in the world. In other worlds, Edwards is showing that these acts of redemption are missional in nature.

This example shows how Edwards's theological treatises reveal missional priorities. Edwards's *The End for Which God Created the World* is selected because of its argument, purpose, and scope of missional themes. As Gibson writes, "Edwards argues that God's chief end in the creation of the world is glorifying himself through his creatures delighting in him forever."[40] Thus, the entire created order was meant to bring glory to God—-including the unbeliever.

Chapter Two

This chapter, entitled "The Universal Depravity of Man," highlights the need for a theology of mission, as it examines the theme of Edwards's view of the fall and corruption of mankind. Since all are sinful, they stand guilty before a holy God and in need of salvation. Similar to the doctrine of God's sovereignty, the doctrine of original sin and human depravity is obviously not unique to Edwards. Yet, Edwards presented the doctrine in a unique way. He defends the notion that all of mankind is born with an innate corrupt disposition. Adam's sin is imputed to the person, not by a passive credit to their account by God, but by an active concurrence with it. As soon as persons come into existence, they take possession of Adam's sin as their own. This condition is evidenced by the fact that all people sin. Regardless of age, race, gender, or nationality, all people stand equally condemned, spiritually dead in their sins. They are wholly unable to do anything that would contribute to their own salvation. Edwards places this doctrine within a missional framework. In other words, the doctrine is cast

---

[39]Edwards quotes specific verses that draw this theme out. Also, his commentary on those verses provide a window into his missional thinking. For just one example, Edwards says that God desires to make his excellencies and perfections known among the nations. He quotes Isaiah 60:6 and says that it is "speaking of the conversion of the Gentile nations to true religion." Furthermore, he selectively cites Isaiah 66:19, highlighting certain phrases, "I will send ... unto the nations ... and to the isles afar off, that have not *heard my fame,* neither have seen my glory; and they shall *declare* my *glory* among the Gentiles." Edwards is drawing out missional themes from these passages. God will work to bring his glory to the Gentile nations. Ibid., 496. Italics original.

[40]Gibson, "Jonathan Edwards: A Missionary?" 395.

with the non-Christian nations in mind. The nations are intrinsically tied to the *telos* of God's redemptive purposes in the world. The gentile, polite men of western society who have not been born again are just as equally lost as the unbeliever who lives outside of civilized society. He writes, "With respect to *every* man, born of the race of Adam, by ordinary generation, that *unless he be born again, he cannot see the kingdom of God.* This is true, not only of the heathen, but of them that are born of the professing people of God, as Nicodemus, and the Jews, and every man born of the flesh."[41]

While much of this chapter focuses on Edwards's treatise *Original Sin,* Edwards develops his doctrine of human depravity in a variety of other places—-most notably, his "Miscellanies." Edwards's work *Original Sin* provides the reason for God's needing to redeem the world. Some scholars have already noted these connections. Jonathan Gibson and Rachel Wheeler briefly note some links in this treatise to world mission, as it established an impetus for engagement with other cultures.[42] As this works was written while he lived among the Stockbridge Indians, Edwards's Reformed views on God's sovereignty and total depravity were reinforced within a cross-cultural context. He was able to shape his thoughts on this doctrine as he ministered to the Native American population. This treatise provides a theological anthropology which establishes actual need for God's redemptive work in world history.

Chapter Three

This chapter, entitled "The Universal Ability and Inability of Man," looks to establish the possibility of salvation within Edwards's theology of world mission. Here, we aim to draw out the distinctly Edwardsian themes of universal ability and inability. This theme also falls broadly under the rubric of theological anthropology. Inevitably, there are some overlapping connections with the previous chapter. Yet, this chapter is distinct in its attempt to articulate the prospect to meet that need for salvation. Fundamental to this concept is the notion that human beings, regardless of their background, race, age, or nationality, are naturally able to repent and believe. There is nothing physically preventing them from choosing the good. No outside

---

[41] Jonathan Edwards, *Original Sin,* ed. Clyde A. Holbrook, vol. 3 of *The Works of Jonathan Edwards* [*WJE*] (New Haven: Yale University Press, 1970), 370.

[42] Gibson, "Jonathan Edwards: A Missionary?" 396. See Rachel Wheeler, "Lessons from Stockbridge: Jonathan Edwards and the Stockbridge Indians," in *Jonathan Edwards at 300: Essays on the Tercentenary of his Birth,* eds. Harry S. Stout, Kenneth P. Minkema, and Caleb J. D. Maskell (New York: University Press of America, 2005), 135.

force is preventing them from repentance and belief. God is not responsible placing humanity in an inescapable problem that is outside their naturally ability to answer. However, men willfully choose to rebel. They will not repent because of a principled resolve to reject Christ. They do not want to choose righteousness. In other words, there is nothing preventing humanity from belief in Christ and doing righteous deeds, but they obstinately dissent out of an unwilling heart.

Edwards's *Freedom of the Will* shows missional themes as it relates to God's sovereignty in creation. In one important argument, Edwards seeks to defend the Reformed doctrine of God's omniscience. He puts forth numerous arguments, maintaining God has certain future knowledge of the will of his moral agents. In his attempt to summarize this point, Edwards writes, "'Tis represented often in Scripture, that God who made the world for himself, and created it for his pleasure, would infallibly obtain his end in the creation, and in all his works; that as all things are *of* him, so they would all be *to* him; and that in the final issue of things, it would appear that he is the first, and the last."[43] In other words, Edwards writes that God's intended redemptive *telos* for the world will ultimately be accomplished by means of the communication of God's glory. Edwards says that the gospel is "effectual for the turning of the non-Christian nations from their heathen apostasy."[44]

Chapter Four

This chapter, entitled "The Verbal Proclamation of the Gospel," highlights Edwards's teaching on the need of a verbal articulation of the gospel message. This provides the method for his theology of mission. The only way by which the Christian religion advances in the world is through the verbal communication of the gospel. Although Edwards believes that there are certain political, economic, and sociological factors that can cultivate growth, the Christian religion is spread through a gospel witness. Here, we evaluate a broad range of revival writings, personal writings, and other treaties.

In the first section of this chapter, we survey the principle narrative works of Edwards. These works provide a wider scope for Edwards's theology of mission, providing the broad scope of how the advancement of the Christian religion in the world takes place. *The Life of David Brainerd* shows how Edwards promoted mission through a biographical account.

---

[43] Jonathan Edwards, *Freedom of the Will,* ed. Paul Ramsey, vol. 1 of *The Works of Jonathan Edwards* [*WJE*] (New Haven: Yale University Press, 1957), 256.

[44] Ibid.

"Brainerd firmly believed, nevertheless, in the mission task. Like Edwards, he held that contact with the Indians was a means by which the glory of the church might be spread."[45] Besides the obvious stories of inspiring personal piety, this narrative reveals much about the practical out workings of Edwards's theological formulas and ministerial strategies involved in the missionary endeavor, most notably through the verbal proclamation of the gospel message.[46] Edwards explicitly intends for Brainerd's life to serve as an example to others, inspiring many to take up a life of missionary service that they, too, might be ambassadors of the gospel.[47] When the missional themes of this work are extracted and explained, we gain a better understanding of how Edwards sees his missional theology being lived out in history.[48] Furthermore, Edwards's *Some Thoughts* provides a larger scale picture of his revival theology. This work directly intersects with missional themes, especially insofar as it promotes the missionary enterprise.[49] This work provides a theology of conversion cast within a schema of a divine contest—the forces of God battling against the forces of Satan. As is often missed in talking about Edwards's revival theology, he frequently speaks in missional language. In other words, he is always aware of the global

---

[45] Norman Pettit, "Editor's Introduction," in Jonathan Edwards, *The Life of David Brainerd*, ed. Norman Pettit, vol. 7 of *The Works of Jonathan Edwards* [*WJE*] (New Haven: Yale University Press, 1984), 1. See Ernest A. Payne, "The Evangelical Revival and the Beginnings of the Modern Missionary Movement" *Congregational Quarterly* 21 (1943): 223–36. Payne charts the influence of Edwards's *An Humble Attempt* and *The Life of David Brainerd* upon early Baptists.

[46] Joseph Conforti notes the multiple literary styles within the work, all of which uniquely contribute to the work's overall function in promoting mission. See Joseph Conforti, "David Brainerd and the Nineteenth Century Missionary Movement," in *Journal of the Early Republic* 5 (1985): 309–32.

[47] Norman Pettit writes, "The diary revealed a perfect example of authentic spirituality." Norman Pettit, "Editor's Introduction," In Jonathan Edwards, *The Life of David Brainerd*, WJE 7:6; See James Manor, "The Coming of Britain's Age of Empire and Protestant Mission Theology, 1750–1839," *Zeitschrift für Missionswissenschaft und Religionswissenschaft* 61 (1977): 38–54; See Wilson H. Kimnach, ed. *Three Essays in Honor of the Publication of "The Life of David Brainerd."* (New Haven: Winthrop Brainerd, 1985); See Stuart Piggin, "The Expanding Knowledge of God: Jonathan Edwards's Influence on Missionary Thinking and Promotion," in *Jonathan Edwards at Home and Abroad: Historical Memories, Cultural Movements, Global Horizons*, ed. David W. Kling and Douglas A. Sweeney (Columbia: University of South Carolina Press, 2003), 266–96.

[48] See Andrew F. Walls, "Missions and Historical Memory: Jonathan Edwards and David Brainerd," *Jonathan Edwards at Home and Abroad: Historical Memories, Cultural Movements, Global Horizons*, ed. David W. Kling and Douglas A. Sweeney (Columbia: University of South Carolina Press, 2003), 248–65.

[49] Arthur Fawcett connects Scottish pastors who took up missional themes from Edwards's call for prayer in *Some Thoughts*. See Arthur Fawcett, *The Cambuslang Revival: The Scottish Evangelical Revival of the Eighteenth Century* (London: Banner of Truth Trust, 1971), 223–30.

progress of the gospel. For example, in this work, Edwards talks about the national implications of imminent revival. He writes that this national revival would probably begin in America.[50] Although considerable scholarly debate has occurred over Edwards's meanings here, one thing that has often been lost in the noise of discussions is the ethno-religious dimension. Edwards denies the suggestion that biblical prophecy is talking about the conversion of Europe alone.[51] When he talks about America "probably" being the referent, he is using that term as shorthand for non-Christian nations being filled with the knowledge of the glory of the Lord. The direct referent Edwards has in mind here is the Native American tribes of North America. This interpretation directly coincides with our attempt to draw out missional themes.

In the second section of this chapter, we will provide a missional reading of Edwards's *An Humble Attempt*. In this work, Edwards advocated for a transnational prayer movement among churches, especially among its leadership. He called on churches, pastors, and laypeople to pray for spiritual awakening. He hoped God would work powerfully in bringing about his purposes in the world. In his conclusion to the work, Edwards reflects, "I hope, [this agreement to pray] ... shall serve greatly to animate and encourage 'em to go on in united prayers for the advancement of Christ's kingdom, with increasing fervency."[52] Edwards clearly anticipates that Christ's kingdom would make progress in the world. Drawing out the full missional implications of this work allows us to see the nature, scope, and method of God's redemptive purposes.[53]

---

[50] Jonathan Edwards, "Some Thoughts Concerning the Present Work of Revival" in *The Great Awakening*, ed. C. C. Goen, vol. 4 of *The Works of Jonathan Edwards* [WJE] (New Haven: Yale University Press, 1972), 353–58.

[51] Edwards is specifically referring to Isaiah 60:9 here. "For the coastlands shall hope for me, the ships of Tarshish first, to bring your children from afar, their silver and gold with them, for the name of the Lord your God, and for the Holy One of Israel, because he has made you beautiful."

[52] Jonathan Edwards, "An Humble Attempt" in *Apocalyptic Writings*, ed. Stephen J. Stein, vol. 5 of *The Works of Jonathan Edwards* [WJE] (New Haven: Yale University Press, 1977), 436.

[53] Oliver Wendell Elsbree connects Edwards's writing to the formation of the Particular Baptist Society for the Promulgation of the Gospel Among the Heathen. See Oliver Wendell Elsbree, *The Rise of the Missionary Spirit in America, 1790–1815* (Williamsport, PA: Williamsport Printing & Binding Co., 1928), 135–36. Also, Earnst Payne looks at the influence Edwards's *An Humble Attempt* made on later prayer revivals and formation of the numerous missionary societies. See Ernest A. Payne, *The Prayer Call of 1784* (London: Baptist Laymen's Missionary Movement, 1941), 4–11.

An analysis of these works will show how Edwards conceived of the advancement of the Christian religion in non-Christian nations. A coherent theology emerges as we continue to draw out images and patterns from Edwards's missional language.

Chapter Five

In this chapter, entitled "The Conversion of the Heart," we close our comprehensive analysis of Edwards's theology of world mission with the final theme of the conversion of the heart. This aspect provides the nature of that theology. What does true Christian religion look like? Since we have broadly defined mission as the advancement of the Christian religion, we must have a proper understanding of the sum and substance of true Christian belief. For Edwards, he saw authentic Christian faith in the heart. Here, we provide a systematic analysis of how Edwards viewed the relationship between the progress of the Christian faith and the personal piety of the believer.

Edwards's *Distinguishing Marks* and other relevant works are analyzed for how they define the limits of authentic Christian spirituality. Because the work of God can sometimes be disguised and misinterpreted, Edwards clarifies what he means by true religion. In other words, the progress of Christian religion must be properly defined in order to be properly measured and evaluated. Edwards provides an analysis of some common misconceptions of what authentic Christian faith really looks like by giving negative signs. These signs are things from which we can draw no real conclusions. These signs are such things like intense emotional reactions or powerful physical manifestations. Then, he provides positive signs, which reveal the core of his theology of heart conversion. This pattern of analysis is a similar pattern which he fully elaborates on in our selected work—the *Religious Affections*. In both of these works, Edwards's regularly connects his argument to a theology of world mission. For one positive sign of authentic religious affection, he writes, "Truly gracious affections are attended with a reasonable and spiritual conviction of the judgment, of the reality and certainty of divine things."[54] Under this heading, he remarks that even the poor non-Christian nations are capable of attaining to simple reason. They do not need to be schooled in European logic and reasoning before they are able to profess authentic faith in Christ. He writes regarding these people,

---

[54] Jonathan Edwards, *Religious Affections*, ed. John E. Smith, vol. 2 of *The Works of Jonathan Edwards* [*WJE*] (New Haven: Yale University Press, 1959), 291.

INTRODUCTION

> If men who have been brought up in heathenism, must wait for a clear and certain conviction of the truth of Christianity, till they have learning and acquaintance with the histories of politer nations, enough to see clearly the force of such kind of arguments; it will make the evidence of the gospel, to them, immensely cumbersome, and will render the propagation of the gospel among them, infinitely difficult. Miserable is the condition of the Houssatunnuck Indians, and others, who have lately manifested a desire to be instructed in Christianity; if they can come at no evidence of the truth of Christianity, sufficient to induce 'em to sell all for Christ, in no other way but this.[55]

Edwards goes on to explain that the gospel of heart conversion is available to all people, regardless of their ethnic or social background. This work in particular will provide us an exemplary account of Edwards's theology of world mission.

Conclusion

We will conclude our study by summarizing the work and providing a systematic organization for the missional themes. It will harmonize the previous chapters' research and present the findings as an integrated whole.

A Case Study in Edwards's Theology of Mission

In this section, we will briefly present a sermon delivered by Edwards to demonstrate our approach. This sermon was one of Edwards's first messages delivered to the Stockbridge Indians. Delivered in the Winter of 1751, it is entitled "The Things That Belong to True Religion." Wilson Kimnach says in his editorial introduction to the sermon, "Indeed, his prospective relationship with the Indians, as well as his doctrine, is artfully encapsulated in this brief sermon."[56] Thus, we can anticipate that this sermon will display his theology as it relates to the theme of world mission.

Edwards's sermon begins by connecting his present audience with past generations of people who have received the gospel message and therein

---

[55] Edwards, *Freedom of the Will*, WJE 1:292.

[56] Jonathan Edwards, "The Things That Belong to True Religion" in *Sermons and Discourses: 1743–1758*, ed. Wilson H. Kimnach, vol. 25 of *The Works of Jonathan Edwards* [WJE] (New Haven: Yale University Press, 2006), 568.

advanced the Christian religion through their faith in Christ. This progress stretches back to the Hebrew prophets, down to Christ and the Apostles, then to European nations, and now to the Stockbridge Indians. Edwards points out how this growth of the Christian gospel comes in direct response to the command of Christ, "After Christ was crucified and rose from the dead, he bid his disciples go and preach the gospel to other nations besides the Jews: to go all over the world and to teach the true religion."[57] Edwards says that Cornelius was a not a Jew, but a Gentile. However, Cornelius was willing to be instructed and prayed to God, asking him for the truth of divine revelation. Upon Peter's preaching, Cornelius came to faith in Christ. Similarly, later Christian ministers preached the gospel in different areas of the world, and the Christian faith was expanded into new non-Christian lands. Edwards then makes his evangelistic appeal, asking them to believe on the Lord Jesus Christ. Putting his message in contrast to the Roman Catholic missionaries, Edwards makes sure to say that true religion does not consist of man-made practices (even of the Protestant variety). True religion consists of having a new heart given to them by God. It involves repenting of sin and having faith in Christ. The result of this heart change is a life transformation whereby one begins to keep the commandments of God. Edwards writes, "They must have their eyes opened to see how lovely Christ is and that he is just such a Savior as such poor creatures as they want. And their hearts must go to Christ."[57] The things that do not belong to true religion involve all efforts at moral self-improvement to achieve salvation. But the things that belong to God are to be found in the inward heart change of a person. Edwards writes in the simplest of terms, "God sees the heart and he looks at the heart."[58] All men are born in sin and they do not have a heart for God. It must be given to them by God. Moreover, Satan will do his best to keep the non-Christian nations in bondage. Yet, Edwards proposes that anyone can pray to God, seeking the things that belong to true religion.

Matching this sermon to our simple definition of mission, the connection is quite apparent. This is an evangelistic sermon intent on advancing the Christian religion in the world through the conversation of the unbeliever. This sermon gives us an excellent window into Edwards's theology of mission. Not only does he broadly sketch how the Christian religion has advanced in the world, he provides the means by which it will continue to progress–

---

[57] Ibid., 570.

[57] Ibid., 572.

[58] Ibid., 573.

namely, the proclamation of the gospel into non-Christian lands. Upon conversion and obedience to the commandments of God, people and nations will be saved. It is not by obedience to outward rituals that one is saved, but only through an inward heart change.

    This sermon clearly outlines a theology of mission by its inclusion of the five themes listed earlier. In such a short message, we see traces of all five of our criterion. First, God's sovereignty is articulated. God rules over human history. At first, God worked through the people of Israel to bring about true religion in the world. Then, God worked though the twelve Apostles, of whom Peter was one. Now, God works through his ministers to advance the Christian religion in the world. Second, there is the need for salvation. All men are depraved and in need of God's saving mercy. Edwards says, "Men must see what poor, miserable creatures they be, and can't help themselves, and [that] they need Christ to pity and help 'em and be their Savior."[59] Without Christ's intervention in their life, men are lost in their sin. Moreover, they need to personally acknowledge their need of salvation and outside intervention. Third, Edwards's message preaches as if they are capable of belief. On the one hand, they are called to follow in the footsteps of Cornelius. On the other hand, "They must have their eyes opened to see how lovely Christ is."[60] They must repent and God is in control of enabling that action. Fourth, this message shows Edwards's belief in the verbal proclamation of the gospel. He writes, "Now I am come to preach the true religion to you and to your children, as Peter did to Cornelius and his family, that you and all your children may be saved. And I hope that you will mind what I say to you, and joyfully receive my words as Cornelius did the words of Peter."[61] The way that they are saved is through conscious faith in Christ. Fifth, their conversion must be an inward, heart belief. They can not simply reject their non-Christian practices and adopt new behaviors. The way in which they experience conversion (and thereby the Christian religion advances) is through an inward transformation of the heart. They repent of their sins and place their faith wholly in Christ for salvation. Edwards writes, "And their hearts must go to Christ. They must come to Christ with all their hearts to save 'em."[62]

---

[59] Ibid., 572.

[60] Ibid., 572.

[61] Ibid., 571.

[62] Ibid., 572.

Conclusion

After giving a brief missional reading of various parts of the Edwardsian corpus, Jonathan Gibson summarizes,

> When the strands of Edwards's theological web are connected we see the prominence of missions: God is glorified when fallen creatures enjoy him forever by delighting in the communication of his love and holiness. This goal is accomplished through communicating God's redemptive work in Christ, which is necessary in the first place because people are unable by themselves to attain knowledge of such things. The chief work of God to accomplish his chief end is the work of redemption, and this work is realized by the means of the missionary preaching to all nations–Native Americans included![63]

This brief sketch provides a window into Edwards's theology of mission. The Christian religion will make its progress throughout the world by means of the communication of the gospel message.

In their preface to the first printed edition in London of Edwards's *Faithful Narrative,* John Guyse and Isaac Watts confidently declared, "Our blessed Lord [will] make a full accomplishment of all his predictions concerning his kingdom, and [will] spread his dominion from sea to sea, through all the nations of the earth."[64] God will one day "awaken whole countries of stupid and sleeping sinners, and kindle divine life in their souls."3 Edwards's narrative of the awakenings in New England stirred the passions of an international community. His theology presented an optimistic view of the future where God's glory would go forth beyond Christendom and into non-Christian lands. In the end, "Salvation shall spread through all the tribes and ranks of mankind."[65]

---

[63] Gibson, "Jonathan Edwards: A Missionary?" 397.

[64] John Guyse and Isaac Watts, "Preface to the First Edition," in Jonathan Edwards, *The Great Awakening,* WJE 4:132.

[65] Ibid., 133.

Chapter 1
The Sovereignty of God

This chapter begins our evaluation of the core tenants of Edwards's theology of mission. Of our two major sections, the first will be a historical-theological analysis of Edwards's foundational component—-the sovereignty of God. Here, we pull from the entire Edwardsian corpus to locate the intersection between his doctrine of the sovereignty of God and the theme of world mission. The second section of this chapter will present a missional reading of Edwards's representative work for this doctrine—*Concerning the End for Which God Created the World*. This approach presents a reading of the text which draws out ideas that contribute to a theology of mission. Again, our definition of mission places the advancement of the Christian religion at the center, especially when it involves those outside of Christendom.

Our argument in this chapter is that Edwards's doctrine of the sovereignty of God was often cast in distinctly missional terms. We will see that Edwards wrote about God's sovereignty with an emphasis on the advancement of the kingdom of Christ on earth. When Edwards brings the theme of world mission and the sovereignty of God into dialogue with one another, he establishes a foundation for his theology of mission. Since God is absolutely sovereign over all things, he will work in history to progressively reconcile all things to himself. The climax of this reconciliation is the salvation of a people from every tongue, tribe, nation, and people group. Necessary to that history of redemption is the conversion of the unbeliever. When God has brought about that global salvation, it will prove that he is able to fulfill his promises, vindicating his sovereignty over the entire world.

The Foundation of a Theology of Mission: A Historical-Theological Survey

Again, our claim is that Jonathan Edwards articulated his doctrine of the sovereignty of God with distinctly missional language. He regularly returned to the theme that God sovereignly works in time and space to bring his redemptive purposes to actualization. This working especially includes the conversion of the unbeliever. Edwards's view of God's sovereignty broadly falls within the Reformed tradition's emphasis on divine authority.[1] This view accentuated the authority of God over all things, such that nothing is outside of his control and rule. Everything that is within his will to do is able to be achieved. For Edwards, mission would be impossible without God's absolute rule and authority over all things. Since God reigns over all things—human agency included—God can sovereignly bring about his purposes in human history.

From the beginning of his public ministry, Jonathan Edwards focused his attention on the dichotomy between the doctrine of the sovereignty of God and its relationship with humankind. In his first ever published work, a sermon entitled *God Glorified in Man's Dependence,* Edwards sought to defend the notion that God is totally sovereign over all things, especially the salvation of men. Therefore, men are to humbly submit themselves to God in dependence upon him.[2] "The redeemed have all their good of God. God is the great author of it; he is the first cause of it, and not only so, but he is the only proper cause."[3] God is the source and fountain of all that is good. Conversely, men are dependent on God for everything, including their conversion. Edwards writes, "We are dependent on the power of God to convert us, and give faith in Jesus Christ, and the new nature."[4] This sermon began a work that would continue throughout his career–namely,

---

[1] This claim is counter to some recent assertions that Edwards departed from this theological tradition. See Jeffrey C. Waddington, "Calvinism," in *The Jonathan Edwards Encyclopedia,* eds. Harry S. Stout, Kenneth P. Minkema, and Adriaan C. Neele (Grand Rapids, MI.: Eerdmans, 2017).

[2] While the title of this sermon should indicate this concept, the doctrine explicitly does so. It reads, *"God is glorified in the wisdom of redemption in this, that there appears in it so absolute and universal a dependence of the redeemed on him."* Jonathan Edwards, "God Glorified in Man's Dependence," in *Sermons and Discourses: 1730–1733,* ed. Mark Valeri, vol. 17 of *The Works of Jonathan Edwards* [WJE] (New Haven: Yale University Press, 1999), 202.

[3] Ibid.

[4] Ibid., 205.

an articulation of the sovereignty of God in its relationship to humankind. This teaching would form the basis for his theology of world mission.

In our evaluation of Edwards's doctrine of the sovereignty of God, we may locate its intersection with world mission under three major themes. First, Edwards saw this foundation of divine sovereignty in mission within a rubric of Trinitarian communication. The love that God has within himself (*ad intra*) emanates outward (*ad extra*). When this love is properly received by the creature, it is returned back to God in worship. Therein, God delights in himself in the creature's reflection of that love. Second, his vision of world mission was cast within a redemptive-historical framework. Edwards saw all of human history as under the sovereign rule and reign of God. The world and all its inhabitants are progressively moving towards an eschatological hope in which the kingdom of Christ on earth would inevitably encompass the ends of the earth. Third, the entire created order was created for the purpose of expanding God's glory among the nations. God created the world so that his perfections might be communicated to people from all nations.

Trinitarian Communication as Missional

The love between the Father and the Son, which is held together by the Holy Spirit, is perfect and complete.[5] God, being the source of all things, communicates his love to the world by a sending forth of that intra-Trinitarian love.[6] In other words, the beginning and source of all love is God. His love to the world originates from within himself. From that source is a well-spring of love that goes out to his creatures.[7] This communication of love is the reason God created the world. He wanted to extend his glory beyond himself to share his glory with ones outside himself. "The infinite

---

[5]For an extensive analysis of this claim, see Robert Caldwell, *Communion in the Spirit: The Holy Spirit as the Bond of Union in the Theology of Jonathan Edwards,* Studies in Evangelical History and Thought (Eugene, OR: Wipf and Stock, 2007).

[6]The nature of this intra-Trinitarian love communicated to the creature will be looked at in more depth in chapter six. The point here is to say that God's mission to the creature originates from within his own self-love.

[7]God's sovereign action in history is likened to a fountain throughout Edwards's writings. In the following quote, we see God's love issuing from him and returning back to him. "I need not run the parallel between this and the course of God's providence through all ages, from the beginning to the end of the world, when all things shall have their final issue in God, the infinite, inexhaustible fountain whence all things come at first, as all the rivers come from the sea, and whither they all shall come at last: for of him and to him are all things, and he is the Alpha and Omega, the beginning and the end." Jonathan Edwards, *Typological Writings,* ed. Wallace E. Anderson, vol. 11 of *The Works of Jonathan Edwards* [WJE] (New Haven: Yale, 1993), 79.

love which there is from everlasting between the Father and the Son is the highest excellency and peculiar glory of the Deity. God saw it therefore meet that there should be some bright and glorious manifestation made of [it] to the creatures, which is done in the incarnation and death of the Son of God."[8] God saw it fit that the love that he shares within himself be communicated outside himself. This love is translated into a "peculiar glory" which is communicated to the creature. Since all glory is due to God, that glory can not find its terminal destination in the creature.[9] So, that communicated glory inevitably returns to him by way of a reflection.[10] The result is God being glorified in the worship of his people.

God's receiving all glory is parallel to his total involvement in salvation. It is planned by God the Father, secured by Christ, and applied to the creature by the indwelling of the Holy Spirit.[11] Edwards is explicit in his articulation of salvation that it is achieved by each member of the Trinity.[12] God's saving purpose in creation is for the expansion of his glory into the world. Edwards writes, "When God had a mind to save men, Christ infinitely laid out himself that the honor of God's majesty might be safe and that God's glory might be advanced."[13] This is explicitly missional language. The advancement of God's glory is necessarily into non-Christian lands. The progress of

---

[8] Jonathan Edwards, *"Miscellanies no. 327[a]" in "The Miscellanies": (Entry Nos. a-z, aa-zz, 1–500)*, ed. Thomas A. Schafter, vol. 13 of *The Works of Jonathan Edwards [WJE]* (New Haven: Yale University Press, 1994), 406.

[9] Edwards says in one of his "Miscellanies," "Wisdom of God in the work of redemption appearing in God's so ordering of it, that man should in everything be so absolutely, immediately and apparently dependent on God, so that God alone should be exalted." Edwards, "Miscellanies no. 486" *WJE* 13:528.

[10] This is the central thesis of Seng-Kong Tan's dissertation. Seng-Kong Tan, *Fullness Received and Returned: Trinity and Participation in Jonathan Edwards*, Emerging Scholars Series (Minneapolis: Fortress Press, 2014); Edwards uses the terms emanation and remanation to communicate this sending and returning of divine glory. Edwards, "End For Which God Created the World" in *Ethical Writings*, ed. Paul Ramsey, vol. 8 of *The Works of Jonathan Edwards [WJE]* (New Haven: Yale University Press, 1989), 531.

[11] A noteworthy point about Edwards's Trinitarianism is that the work of each member of the Trinity is part of what distinguishes their personhood. After describing the saving work of the Father and Son, he writes, "Hereby was most clearly manifested to men and angels the distinction of the persons of the Trinity." See Edwards, "Miscellanies no. 327[a]" *WJE* 13:406.

[12] Edwards's emphasis on the Trinity in salvation can be viewed in light of eighteenth century polemics against the Trinity by Deists and Socinians. For Edwards, a proper theology of mission must take a distinctly Trinitarian shape.

[13] Edwards, "Miscellanies no. 327[a]" *WJE* 13:406.

God's glory communicated to the world is meant to extend to all nations.[14] Moreover, the future hope of gospel progress does not ultimately rely on the work of men, it is assured by the promise of God.[15] This fact is why God can rightly receive all the glory for this work. Still, this advancement lays within God's sovereign will. Therefore, one must pray to God, which is an exercise of dependence on him. Fervent prayer and intercession to God might be a catalyst to a worldwide gospel movement.[16]

Furthermore, the vision Edwards casts for his readers is one of successful gospel progress that would extend to the furthest reaches of the globe. Commenting on Isaiah 11:9, Edwards writes,

> Which is as much as to say, as there is no place in the vast ocean where there is not water, so there shall be no part of the world of mankind where there is not the knowledge of the Lord; as there is no part of the wide bed or cavity possessed by the sea, but what is covered with water, so there shall be no part of the habitable world, that shall not be covered by the light of the gospel, and possessed by the true religion.[17]

The other religions, idols, false gods, and systems that are opposed to the Christian religion will be destroyed and the Christian religion will prevail.

---

[14] One of the places where this idea is seen clearest is Edwards's *An Humble Attempt*. This discourse is a call for lay people and ministers on both sides of the Atlantic to engage in earnest prayer for spiritual awakening. Edwards says that the advancement of the kingdom of Christ in this world is ensured by God. Edwards writes, "It is evident from the Scripture, that there is *yet remaining* a great advancement of the interest of religion and the kingdom of Christ in this world, by an abundant outpouring of the Spirit of God, far greater and more extensive than ever yet has been." Jonathan Edwards, "An Humble Attempt" in *Apocalyptic Writings: "Notes on Apocalypse," An Humble Attempt,* ed. Stephen J. Stein, vol. 5 of *The Works of Jonathan Edwards* [*WJE*] (New Haven: Yale, 1977), 330.

[15] Mark Rogers writes, "For Edwards, the future advancement of Christ's kingdom was not just a speculative dream. The prophecies of the Bible, particularly the book of Revelation, provided detailed description of how God's work of redemption would continue and culminate in the future." Rogers then goes on to note Edwards's commentary on the book of Revelation. He sees its existence as evidence of Edwards's belief in the accuracy of divine prophecy. Mark C. Rogers, "A Missional Eschatology: Jonathan Edwards, Future Prophecy, and the Spread of the Gospel," *Fides et Historia* 41 (2009): 23.

[16] Although the entire treatise *An Humble Attempt* assumes that one must pray to God because God has the power to work change in the world, his sermon "Christian Safety" explicitly says so.

[17] Edwards, "An Humble Attempt" *WJE* 5:332; Isaiah 11:9, "They shall not hurt nor destroy in all my holy mountain: for the earth shall be full of the knowledge of the Lord, as the waters cover the sea."

The knowledge of God will extend to the furthest reaches of the globe. He writes, "There will not be one nation remaining in the world, which shall not embrace the true religion."[18] Ultimately, God will see that his glory is spread throughout the world. However, the means by which that dissemination of glory will happen is through the verbal witness of his church. As that gospel message makes progress in the world, the power of Satan will gradually erode, and it will eventually be completely destroyed.[19] Therefore, the church will be instrumental in giving Christ the glory he rightfully deserves. He writes,

> It is natural and reasonable to suppose, that the whole world should finally be given to Christ, as one whose right it is to reign, as the proper heir of him, who is originally the king of all nations, and the possessor of heaven and earth: and the Scripture teaches us, that God the Father hath constituted his Son, as God-man, and in his kingdom of grace, or mediatorial kingdom, to be "the heir of the world," that he might in this kingdom have "the heathen for his inheritance, and the utmost ends of the earth for his possession" (Heb. 1:2 and 2:8; Ps. 2:6–8).[20]

Here we see the connection between divine sovereignty and missional language. He is rightfully the possessor of heaven and earth. This is the language of divine sovereignty in action. He is originally the king of all nations and the heir of the world who will have the unbeliever for his inheritance. This is the language of world mission. Edwards believed that God's sovereign rule and reign would be the ground for the hope of missional progress. God is worthy to be praised by all of his creation. Thus, he sees

---

[18] Ibid.

[19] God vindicates his name by triumphing over the false gods and idols of the nations. Edwards illustrates this point well in an extended reflection in one of his "Miscellanies" entitled "Christian Religion. Fulfillment of the Prophecies of Messiah in the Conversion of the Gentiles from Heathenism by the Means of Jesus." Here, Edwards highlights God's being exalted and glorified in the destruction of false religions. Edwards writes, "So God is represented in the prophecies of Isaiah as gloriously manifesting himself as above the gods of the heathen, in appearing above Bel and Nebo, the idols of Babylon, when Babylon was destroyed and the Jews delivered from their captivity there." This triumph over the foreign idols would translate into the conversion of the heathen. They would see the errors of their ways, repent, and place their faith in Christ for salvation. This conversion would be to the advancement of the Christian religion. See Jonathan Edwards, "Miscellanies no. 1327" in *The "Miscellanies": (Entry Nos. 1153–1360)*, eds. D. A. Sweeney & H. S. Stout, vol. 23 of *The Works of Jonathan Edwards* [*WJE*] (New Haven: Yale University Press, 2004), 308.

[20] Ibid., 330.

fit to bring his creation into his fullness. From his intra-Trinitarian love, God communicates his love *ad extra* to his creatures. They are invited to participate in that love, which is an advancement of the kingdom of Christ.[21]

God as Sovereign Lord over Human History

Edwards's missiology connects directly with his history of redemption. Edwards preached a series of thirty sermons between March and August 1739, all of which were posthumously published under the title "A History of the Work of Redemption." These sermons were an extended exposition of one verse—-Isaiah 51:8. "For the moth will eat them up like a garment, and the worm will eat them like wool, but my righteousness will be forever, and my salvation to all generations." These sermons were expositions of historical narratives intended to paint a wide picture of God's redemptive work in history. Moreover, they were also meant to locate the hearers within their historical context. Contemporary believers are connected to generations of past saints, and they are ensured a future and a hope. In the present day, they should live their lives in constant awareness of this big picture. George Marsden writes, "The constant motif, as in Edwards' view of nearly everything, was the conflict between God and Satan ... Edwards constantly urged his parishioners towards grand perspectives to help them overcome the pettiness and self-absorption that went with their low horizons."[22] Edwards sought to provide a wider framework for his audience, rooted in Scripture, so that they might live differently.

The path on which Edwards places the reader always has this end in mind–that all nations would eventually come to the knowledge of the glory of God. All nations and people, being made in the image of God, will be represented in God's coming kingdom. Every human soul will have to give an account. The reprobate will be judged and the elect will be redeemed. The remnant, God's elect people, will be saved and the ends of the earth will come to know God's glory and authority. All of the created order is moving toward that final end. In one notable sermon, Edwards says, "[God]

---

[21] Jim Salladin supports the claim that Edwards held to the idea of theosis. While he remained squarely within the Reformed tradition, Edwards held to the doctrine as it was broadly articulated in the Greek Patristic tradition. This doctrine holds that there is a participation in the divine nature, while maintaining a distinction between the creator and the creature. See Jim Salladin, in *The Jonathan Edwards Encyclopedia,* eds. Harry S. Stout, Kenneth P. Minkema, and Adriaan C. Neele (Grand Rapids, MI.: Eerdmans, 2017); This subject will be taken up again and in more detail in chapter six.

[22] George Marsden, *Jonathan Edwards: A Life* (New Haven: Yale University Press, 2003), 194.

holds an absolute and uncontrollable government in the world; and thus he has done from the beginning, and thus he will do to the end of all things. Neither is his dominion confined to the children of men, but he rules the whole creation."[23] Edwards not only interpreted narrative and prophetic literature along these lines, but he also understood the full scope of Scripture chronicling redemptive history.

This idea leads us to understand that Edwards saw every point of Scripture as points on a single path which leads to an ultimate end—-the kingdom of God being expanded to the ends of the earth. Edwards regularly envisions this expansion reaching those outside Christendom. He writes, "Satan's heathenish kingdom be overthrown. Gross heathenism now possesses great part of the earth, and there are supposed to be more heathens now in the world than of all professions put together, Jews, Mohammedans and Christians. But then the heathen nations shall be enlightened with the glorious gospel."[24] In other words, Edwards interpreted the individual parts of Scripture as relating to the whole with history moving towards a definite climax in which God would ultimately vindicate his name in nations.[25] Edwards writes, "Now the kingdom of Christ shall in the most strict and literal sense extend to all nations and the whole earth. There are many passages of Scripture that can be understood in no other sense."[26]

Not only did Edwards have this idea clearly in mind, but he also believed that all Christians should participate in hastening the coming of his kingdom. Edwards articulated this idea clearly in his work *An Humble Attempt,*

> It is evident from the Scripture, that there is *yet remaining* a great advancement of the interest of religion and the kingdom of Christ in this world, by an abundant outpouring of the Spirit of God, far greater and more extensive than ever yet has been.

---

[23] Jonathan Edwards, "God's Excellencies" in *Sermons and Discourses, 1720–1723,* eds. H. Kimnach & H. S. Stout, vol. 10 in *The Works of Jonathan Edwards* [WJE] (New Haven: Yale University Press, 1992), 422.

[24] Edwards, *A History of the Work of Redemption,* vol. 9 of *The Works of Jonathan Edwards* [WJE] (New Haven: Yale, 1989), 471.

[25] Stephen R. C. Nichols argues that Edwards stressed the unity of the Old and New Testament in light of polemics against Deists like Anthony Collins (1676–1729). Where Deists sought to particularly discredit the Old Testament on the grounds of its perceived injustice and violence by God, Edwards sought to defend the Old Testament by linking it with the New. See Stephen R. C. Nichols, *Jonathan Edwards's Bible: The Relationship Between the Old and New Testaments* (Eugene, OR: Pickwick, 2013), 12.

[26] Edwards, *A History of the Work of Redemption,* WJE 9:473.

> 'Tis certain, that many things, which are spoken concerning a glorious time of the church's enlargement and prosperity in the latter days, have never yet been fulfilled.[27]

Drawing heavily from the Old Testament, he anticipates the prospect of advancements in Christendom by which all nations would "embrace the true religion, and be brought into the church of God."[28] Commenting on Revelation 19:6, Edwards envisions a future day that "is so often spoken of in the Psalms and Prophets, of God reigning over all nations."[29] Since God answers the prayers of his people, they should seek him in prayer for the advancement of his kingdom. God will answer his people for prayers like these. God has proven his ability and willingness to answer prayer throughout the history of Israel. Edwards sees many Old Testament events as typifying later events. He writes, "Scripture instances and examples of success in prayer give great encouragement to pray for this mercy. Most of the remarkable deliverances and restorations of the church of God, that we have account of in the Scripture, were in answer to prayer."[30] He says the liberation of God's people from Egyptian bondage was a type of redemption Christ enact for people enslaved in sin. This liberation came in response to prayer. Also, the sun stood still at Gibeon so that God's people would experience military victory over their enemies. Similarly, this victory came in response to prayer. Edwards interprets this event as a type of future spiritual victory that the church would experience. He writes, "God seemed to have some respect to a future more glorious event to be accomplished for the Christian church, in the day of her victory over her enemies, in the latter days."[31]

Edwards is careful to note the international context in which biblical events happen. This presentation style directly corresponds to his theology of world mission. The work of God being wrought before the non-Christian nations is something to attract the nations to God. He especially draws this out when speaking of the Exodus from Egypt and the post-exilic return from captivity.

---

[27] Edwards, "An Humble Attempt" *WJE* 5:329.

[28] Ibid.

[29] Ibid., 123.

[30] Ibid., 355.

[31] Ibid.

> About Moses' time, when truth, that had been upheld by tradition, was very much lost, and former things became much out of sight by being far off, and the professors of the true religion, excepting in the posterity of Jacob, very much ceased in the world, God took care that there might be something new, [which] should be very public, and of great fame, and much taken notice of abroad, in the world heard, that might be sufficient to lead sincere inquirers to the true God; and those were the great things God wrought in Egypt, and at the Red Sea, and in the wilderness, for the children of Israel. Those things were very publicly wrought. Egypt, where many of them were wrought, was one of the most noted heathen nations in the world. And we often read how that those great miracles that God wrought actually were taken notice of by the heathen nations round about; and probably most, if not all, the heathen nations heard of them.[32]

Edwards is insisting that the reader see the Exodus narrative in its geopolitical context. Egypt was a great and powerful nation. In order to awaken the nations to his glory, he miraculously delivered his people in a very public manner. These mighty works were displayed in an overt way that they might be broadcast across the world. The non-Christian nations would be watching, so God decided to reveal his sovereign power and grace in order that the world would take notice. Edwards points the reader to the transnational communication of God's glory. This extraordinary deliverance would strike fear and awe into the nations. God's purpose in his public performance is that his glory would be received.

We can see here and numerous other places that Edwards's history of redemption provides a framework from which to establish a theology of world mission. The hope is that the nations would see God's sovereign working in the world and be drawn into his power and love. Being aware of this missional language in Edwards's account of redemptive history will help us see part of the foundation of his theology of mission, but there is also another remaining component.

---

[32] Jonathan Edwards, *Notes on Scripture*, ed. Stephen J. Stein, vol. 15 of *The Works of Jonathan Edwards* [*WJE*] (New Haven: Yale University Press, 1998), 370.

The Eschatological Hope for the Nations

If the sovereignty of God is the starting point for Edwards's theology of mission, we must also determine its end point. Knowing the beginning and the end will help us to determine what happens in between. Throughout his life, Jonathan Edwards held a vision of eschatological hope.[33] In part, Edwards held that one cataclysmic event—the millennial reign of Christ on earth—-will be an epoch of great divine blessing. This intense period of divine blessing will immediately follow a period where the nations would experience an increasing measure of God's saving mercies. Edwards held steadfast in his belief that the kingdom of Christ will expand on the earth. Those who are in darkness and bondage to the dominion of Satan will be liberated by the communication of the gospel. Moreover, numerous periods of divine blessing will immediately follow intense periods of divine judgment.[34] God will send forth a series of judgments upon the nations of the world for their rejection of gospel truths. The peoples would be liberated from false religions that held them in subjugation.

Edwards's vision of eschatological hope involved missionary activity. The church is to bear witness to the nations of Christ's redemptive work. While only the elect will respond in saving faith, the nations are to be offered the hope of the gospel. One day, this salvation will reach its inevitable destination. Satan's kingdom would inevitably be torn down, and the nations would come to experience salvation. Edwards says the Bible "speaks of the whole earth's being filled with the knowledge and worship of the true God by the preaching of the gospel 'to every nation, and kindred, and tongue, and people,' as attending the downfall and dismal punishment

---

[33] Robert G. Lee succinctly clearly and summarizes Edwards's eschatological position. "Edwards's doctrine of the end times included a thousand-year period of peace and prosperity for the church before the second coming of Christ. His predictions for a glorious period were filled with idealistic, universal, utopian visions of a reign of the church on earth. He was 'postmillennial,' in that he postponed the ultimate coming of Christ until after divine knowledge was diffused to all parts of the globe... His picture of the church was triumphant and progressive such that all the earth would be filled with the glory of God." Robert G. Lee, "Eschatology," in *The Jonathan Edwards Encyclopedia,* eds. Harry S. Stout, Kenneth P. Minkema, and Adriaan C. Neele (Grand Rapids, MI: Eerdmans, 2017).

[34] While this pattern may sound like an endless repetition of judgment and blessing, Edwards's view of history is not purely cyclical. McClymond and McDermott rightly describe Edwards's view like a corkscrew drilling into a surface. When viewed vertically, it appears to be moving in a cyclical pattern, but when viewed horizontally, it appears to be progressing in one direction. See Michael J. McClymond and Gerald R. McDermott, *The Theology of Jonathan Edwards* (New Haven: Yale, 2012), 233.

of Babylon."³⁵ The gospel would go forth and be received by the nations as faithful evangelists share the good news. Edwards writes, "The word εὐαγγελίζονται, 'are evangelized,' implies not only being the subject of the preaching of the gospel, or the telling the good news, but a being encouraged, refreshed, and revived, and made joyful and happy by it."³⁶ The nations will be made happy by the preaching of the gospel. He then says, "The poor's being evangelized is the last effect mentioned, it being that which crowns all, representing the main thing which Jesus came into the world for, the blessed effect that he had respect to in all that he said and did, and the great thing of which the other things here mentioned were but types and representations."³⁷ From the top of society down to its very bottom ("the poor"), God will restore the nations with the preaching of the gospel. This is the eschatological hope of the nations. The path on which Edwards places the reader always has this end in mind—-that all nations would eventually come to the knowledge of the glory of God. All nations and people, being made in the image of God, will be represented in God's coming Kingdom. Therefore, Edwards's history of redemption could just as easily be called a history of mission when we see it in light of its foundational purpose—-namely, God's work of expanding is glory and advancing his kingdom in the world.

In one of Edwards's earliest "Miscellanies," he writes, "For certainly it was the goodness of the Creator that moved him to create; and how can we conceive of another end proposed by goodness, than that he might delight in seeing the creatures he made rejoice in that being that he has given them?"³⁸ God created the world that he might delight in his creature's enjoyment of him. This concept encapsulates what it means to glorify God. To glorify God is to enjoy him. Edwards asks rhetorically, "Now what is glorifying God, but a rejoicing at that glory he has displayed?"³⁹ To delight, enjoy, and rejoice in God is to glorify him. Edwards goes on to say that it is not merely enough to have a mental ascent to this knowledge. One must have a heartfelt devotion to God and his glory. God's creative purposes were intended for all of his creation. God elected the nation of Israel to bless the nations. Similarly, the

---

³⁵ Jonathan Edwards, *The "Blank Bible": Part 1*, ed. Stephen J. Stein, vol. 24 of *The Works of Jonathan Edwards* [*WJE*] (New Haven: Yale University Press, 2006), 805.

³⁶ Ibid, 843.

³⁷ Ibid, 843.

³⁸ Edwards, "Miscellanies no. 3" *WJE* 13:199.

³⁹ Ibid.

church was also blessed to be a blessing to the nation. Edwards's makes this connection between Israel's purpose and the purpose of the church. He comments on the Abrahamic covenant's reaffirmation in Genesis 17, "Several particulars concerning that covenant were revealed more fully than ever had been before, not only that Christ was to be of Abraham's seed but also the calling of the Gentiles and the bringing all nations unto the church. A blessing [of] all the families of the earth was now made known."[40] Abraham was given the promise of seed and blessing. He was blessed by God to be a blessing to all the families of the earth. Specifically, the "calling of the Gentiles and the bringing all nations unto the church" is distinctly missional language. God will bless the nations with the light of the gospel and the kingdom of Christ will be advanced in the world.

Edwards's eschatological hope of the world necessarily involves the non-Christian nations. This "glory of the approaching happy days of the church" means an advancement of the kingdom of God on earth.[41] This third and final point of our historical-theological analysis of Edwards's doctrine of the sovereignty of God establishes a fixed end point for God's working in the world. Thus, there is an eschatological hope for the nations—-that they will be included in the redemptive plan of God.

Concerning the End for Which God Created the World: A Missional Reading

Edwards's dissertation Concerning the *End for Which God Created the World* stands as the leading exemplar of where his doctrine of the sovereignty of God and theology of world mission intersect. Written at the end of his life, this dissertation shows the underpinning of all of Edwards's missional theology, representing the mature thought life of Edwards.[42] In the dissertation, Edwards takes up the purpose, end, and reason for God's creation. Nearly every topic of Edwards's wider theology can be seen as flowing out of this work. Not only does it lay the foundation for creaturely existence, but it also tells us something about the character of God. We can see this dissertation as a "sort of prolegomenon to all his work."[43] The work is so important that it

---

[40] Edwards, *A History of the Work of Redemption*, WJE 9:161.

[41] Jonathan Edwards, "Distinguishing Marks" in *The Great Awakening*, ed. C. C. Goen, vol. 4 of *The Works of Jonathan Edwards* [WJE] (New Haven: Yale University Press, 1972), 278.

[42] Edwards completed his dissertation in 1755.

[43] George Marsden, *Jonathan Edwards: A Life* (New Haven: Yale, 2003), 460.

"might be seen as the logical starting point for all of his thinking."[44] Similarly, Joe Rigney says, "The work is rightly seen as the deepest foundation of all of Edwards's theological and pastoral reflection, and is the culmination of a lifetime of reflection on the question: What is God's purpose in creating the world?"[45] Therefore, we can treat this work as the entryway into which we might begin our study into Edwards's theology of mission.

The inquiry into the purpose of God creating the world was not some abstract attempt to satisfy the curiosity of an esoteric philosopher. The theological milieu in which this question emerges derives from a philosophical shift towards an anthropocentric worldview.[46] In the emerging culture of transatlantic academics, Deists and Arminians began to argue that God's end in creating the world was primarily for the benefit of man.[47] The happiness of the creature was placed at the end of God's creative intent. In other words, God created the world in order that his creatures might be enraptured in eternal felicity and joy. This position was seen in contrast to the Reformed doctrine that placed God at the center.[48] Seen most explicitly in the Westminster Shorter Catechism's first question and answer: "What is the chief and of man? Man's chief end is to glorify God and enjoy him

---

[44] Ibid.

[45] Joe Rigney, "End for Which God Created the World," in *The Jonathan Edwards Encyclopedia*, eds. Harry S. Stout, Kenneth P. Minkema, and Adriaan C. Neele (Grand Rapids, MI.: Eerdmans, 2017).

[46] Mark Noll accurately and succinctly characterizes the period, "For religious thinkers, the parallel shift of meaning was from contemplative theocentricism to activistic anthropocentricism. In Edwards's famous formulation, 'True virtue must chiefly consist in love to God; the Being of beings, infinitely the greatest and best'." Mark A Noll, *America's God: From Jonathan Edwards to Abraham Lincoln* (New York: Oxford University Press, 2002), 440; E. Brooks Holifield also describes the theological shift where some theologians had an "increasing respect for reason." Furthermore, "confidence in the reasonableness of theology was closely tied to a changing estimate of human nature and its moral potential." E. Brooks Holifield, *Theology in America, Christian Thought from the Age of the Puritans to the Civil War* (New Haven: Yale University Press, 2003), 129.

[47] Edwards derided these philosophers, calling them "our modern freethinkers." These would have included such persons as John Toland (1670–1722), Anthony Collins (1676–1729), and Matthew Tindal (1657–1733); Edwards, "End for Which God Created the World" in *Ethical Writings, WJE* 8:536.

[48] This contrast is not to deny that God's glorification and humanity's joy are at odds in the Reformed doctrine. However, the emphasis in the Reformed literature is always on God's glory as supreme. Humanity's joy comes as a byproduct of their placing God at the center of their worship and praise. Therefore, the principle aim is not the creature's joy as supreme, but God's being exalted as supreme.

forever."[49] Thus, according to the tradition, the glory of God is the reason, purpose, and ultimate end of God's creation.[50]

As is typical of Edwards, he takes up the question from a solidly Reformed perspective, yet he answers it in a creative and unique way.[51] Not content with responding with a combative and defensive posture, Edwards addresses the concerns of his opponents while also advancing the traditional doctrines of the Reformed tradition. The essence of Edwards's argument is that God's ultimate end in creating the world is that he might be glorified by his creature's eternal enjoyment in him. This end is achieved by God redeeming his people in history. Therefore, Edwards maintains the Reformed position, but he does so while also incorporating the dissenting view's concern of creaturely happiness.

The first section of his dissertation focuses on defending the logic that God's glory is at the center of his purpose. Here, Edwards guards against contemporary notions that would seek to place creaturely happiness at the center. He defends the Reformed position, purely from a series of logical deductions.[52] The second part of the dissertation is a biblical-theological presentation of the argument. This section also takes up the issue of God's seeking his own glory in the creation of the world. Yet, it also talks about the importance of the method by which this glory is spread about the world––namely, the proclamation of the gospel message.

The first major section determines Jonathan Edwards's larger framework for missions. It bookends his history of redemption and gives an outline for how the advancement of the kingdom of God will take place. Starting with the identity of God as the Creator and sustainer of all things, Edwards places God at the center of his theology of missions. God is all-sufficient

---

[49]Philip Schaff, *The Creeds of Christendom,* vol. 3 (New York: Harper, 1951), 676.

[50]This point can be aptly summarized in the Latin phrase *Soli Deo Gloria,* which means "to the glory of God alone."

[51]McClymond and McDermott write, "As much as any other writing, *End of Creation* illustrated Edwards's unique combination of tradition and innovation in theological reasoning." McClymond and McDermott, *The Theology of Jonathan Edwards,* 207.

[52]For the purposes of his argument, he does not depend on the Scriptural witness to make his case. This approach is an apologetic technique that Edwards employs for the sake of his readers. He fully anticipates that those who do not share his Reformed inclinations would read it and engage its arguments. By using this apologetic technique, Edwards's treatise is missional as it talks about the foundation of his theology of mission. In other words, Edwards is attempting to expand the Christian faith into the arena of unbelieving academics (Deist).

and in need of nothing outside of himself.[53] No creature can add to him. He is fully happy and complete as he enjoys his own glory.[54] The Father glories in the Son and the Holy Spirit is the loving bond that unites them all together.[55] Out of his intra-Trinitarian perfection, he desires to manifest his glory not out of any insufficiency, but out of his own good pleasure.[56] Edwards writes, "If it be thus fit that God should have a supreme regard to himself, then it is fit that this supreme regard should appear, in those things by which he makes himself known, or by his *word* and *works*." [57] This point establishes God's passion for his own glory, for there is nothing higher than it. Further, God desires to make this supreme regard manifest in the world through his word and works. This desire to communicate his glory establishes the beginning of mission. If God has an idea that is perfect in his

---

[53] The creature entirely depends in the Creator for everything, and the Creator does not depend on the creature even in the slightest. Edwards asks rhetorically, "Now, if the creature receives its all from God entirely and perfectly, how is it possible that it should have anything to add to God, to make him in any respect more than he was before, and so the Creator become dependent on the creature?" The answer is obviously a negative response. God is not added to by his creation. Edwards begins his entire theology of mission with a theocentric vision for all of reality. Edwards, "End for Which God Created the World," *WJE* 8:420.

[54] God is not dependent on anything else for his existence because he is eternally happy in himself. Not determined by any external or prior cause, God depends totally on himself. "God is infinitely, eternally, unchangeably, and independently glorious and happy." Whenever he acts, he does so out of his own good pleasure, not out of any external requirement that constrains God. Ibid., 420; Edwards says that God fully delights in his own perfections, "A respect to himself, or an infinite propensity to, and delight in his own glory, is that which causes him to incline to its being abundantly diffused, and to delight in the emanation of it." Ibid., 439.

[55] Both the editorial note in the *WJE* and Joe Rigney pick up on the distinctly Edwardsian Trinitarianism here. There is the fountain of God's glory, a self-knowledge of that glory, and the love that connects the two. These correspond to the Father, Son, and Holy Spirit. This chain of reasoning shows the depth of the doctrine of the Trinity for Edwards. Moreover, it reveals his creative expression of classical doctrines. Ibid., 432; Joe Rigney, "End for Which God Created the World, The (1765)," in *The Jonathan Edwards Encyclopedia,* eds. Harry S. Stout, Kenneth P. Minkema, and Adriaan C. Neele (Grand Rapids, MI.: Eerdmans, 2017).

[56] God is fully and eternally happy within himself and needs nothing to add to his value. He is under no obligation to create. Yet, God did choose to create. All of reality flows out of his existence. God's actions are related to their worth. Joe Rigney explains this point by Edwards, "God operates according to the principle of proportionate regard. That is, this principle, by which a being values things according to their value, is *descriptive* of God, rather than *prescriptive* for God, as though he could be subordinated to an external ethical norm." God is not obliged to act in a way that he does not enjoy. Moreover, he does not inappropriately value things. God does not assign worth to a thing that is unworthy of that regard. These basic principles underline Edwards's missiology in that they establish God as one who is self-sufficient, under no obligation to create, let alone save man from sin and death. Joe Rigney, "End for Which God Created the World, The (1765)," in *The Jonathan Edwards Encyclopedia,* eds. Harry S. Stout, Kenneth P. Minkema, and Adriaan C. Neele (Grand Rapids, MI.: Eerdmans, 2017).

[57] Edwards, "End for Which God Created the World" *WJE* 8:422.

mind (a supreme regard for his own name), it is fitting that the idea should become manifest and appear to the world.

Then God designs that glory to be seen and enjoyed. That the creatures might enjoy and delight in God's glory is the reason God created the world. "If the idea of God's perfection in the understanding be valuable, then the love of the heart seems to be more especially valuable, as moral beauty especially consists in the disposition and affection of the heart."[58] If the creature's beholding the glory of God is an exceptional thing, then how much more exceptional would the creature's love and appreciation of that glory be? In the creature's enjoyment of God, God's purpose in creating is fulfilled.

Edwards's summation is that God created the world so that we might communicate his internal fullness to the creature. He writes,

> It appears reasonable to suppose that it was what God had respect to as an ultimate end of his creating the world, to communicate of his own infinite fullness of good; or rather it was his last end, that there might be a glorious and abundant emanation of his infinite fullness of good *ad extra,* or without himself, and the disposition to communicate himself or diffuse his own *fullness,* which we must conceive of as being originally in God as a perfection of his nature, was what moved him to create the world.[59]

This idea is profoundly missional. God desires to communicate his fullness to the creature. Out of the excellencies he has within himself, he moves to extend that glory outside of himself. This fullness may be equated with his glory. This extension of glory is an advancement of his rule and reign. Although God and his glory are ultimately at the center of his creative purpose, the creature's delight and enjoyment is the means by which this is achieved.[60] The creatures participate in God's intra-Trinitarian enjoyment. God's communication of his glory and love are ultimately returned to him,

---

[58] Ibid., 432.

[59] Ibid., 433–434.

[60] Edwards writes, "God may have a real and proper pleasure or happiness in seeing the happy state of the creature: yet this may not be different from his delight in himself." In other words, God's delight in the creatures is really a delight in his own reflected glory. Edwards vividly likens this idea to how the sun brightens a magnificent jewel. The sun does not become more bright by the jewel's reflection of the sun. It merely participates in the brightness of the sun itself. In the same way, God's glory is not added to by the creature's enjoyment of it. Ibid., 446.

achieving their true destination.[61] This divine purpose is for his elect. Again, this is explicitly missional language. God acts in order to bring about the enjoyment of himself in the world.

Whereas the first section of Edwards's treatise is a philosophical engagement to the question (What is God's purpose in creating the world?), the second part is the biblical-theological answer to the question. Both part one and part two arrive at the same conclusion, but from different perspectives. Here, Edwards considers all of the biblical evidence and analyzes specific Scriptures in detail. He intends to show God's ultimate end in the creation of the world was to magnify his own glory. While Edwards treats numerous passages here, we will take only a few of his examples for the purposes of drawing out wider missional themes.

One example in the beginning of this section is Edwards's reference to Rom. 11:36.[62] Edwards says that Paul's reflection on the following discourse causes him to erupt in praise to God. Edwards writes, "[Paul's] discourse shows how God contrived and brought this to pass in his disposition of things, viz. by setting up the kingdom of Christ in the world; leaving the Jews, and calling the Gentiles; and in what he would hereafter do in bringing in the Jews with the fullness of the Gentiles."[63] The kingdom of Christ was inaugurated in the world in order that the Gentiles might be included in the promises of God. The mighty works of God in the world are wrought so that God's glory might be manifest and magnified. The intent in God's creation is not found in a tribal or parochial focus. The end of God's creative purpose is not found in an ethnic locality. Edwards's point from Rom. 11:36 is that God's creative purpose is found in his own universal, worldwide glorification.

---

[61] Ultimately, God's love to believers is grounded in his love to himself. The Father desired to vindicate his name among the nations, and so he sent his Son to accomplish his mission. Edwards uses the terms *emanation* and *remanation* to communicate this idea. Moreover, Edwards regularly brings out this international context. He writes, "In the creature's knowing, esteeming, loving, rejoicing in, and praising God, the glory of God is both exhibited and acknowledged; his fullness is received and returned. Here is both an emanation and remanation. The refulgence shines upon and into the creature, and is reflected back to the luminary. The beams of glory come from God, and are something of God, and are refunded back again to their original. So that the whole is of God, and in God, and to God; and God is the beginning, middle and end in this affair." Ibid., 531.

[62] "For of him, and through him, and to him, are all things: to whom be glory for ever. Amen." Romans 11:36.

[63] Edwards, "End for Which God Created the World" *WJE* 8:475.

Another example can be found in Edwards's usage of Isa. 43:6–7.[64] Edwards points to this text to support his claim that God's seeking his own glory is also for the good of the entire creation. This texts speaks of the broad scope of God's creative purpose. From both north and south, far away, and to the ends of the earth, God desires everyone who is called by his name is to be included these promises. There is a worldwide scope to God's creative purposes. Edwards's overall point is to say that this desire of God is not selfish in the normal way one associates the word with negative connotations. If a person is self-seeking, he does so to the exclusion and detriment of others. When God seeks his own glory, it actually serves the creatures to their best end, for this is their created purpose. When Edwards references these verses, he does so with the ends of the earth in mind. Edwards's inclusion of verses like Phil. 2:11 also support this reading. But how is this global enjoyment to take effect? Edwards concludes that it will take place through the proclamation of the Gospel in the world. He writes after quoting Rev. 14:6–7, "As though this were the sum and end of that virtue and religion, which was the grand design of preaching the gospel everywhere through the world."[65] God desires to bring glory to himself by making his perfections known. God's act of brining glory to himself is a good which is intended to come through transnational communication of the gospel. Virtue and religion are common to all cultures and nations of the world. They both find their ultimate fulfillment in the one true God and his gospel. It is only the proclamation of that gospel that this purpose is realized in the world.

In a flurry of biblical references, Edwards says that everything God does is ultimately for his own name's sake. Here, we must note the missional emphasis in Edwards's references. In one reference, Edwards cites Ezekiel 20:9 which says that God acted so that he name "should not be polluted before the heathen."[66] Since God's name was being defiled in the sight of the nations, he publically responded so as to restore his honor. This act was a missional response. Edwards also cites Ezekiel 36:21–23 where God promises, "I will *sanctify my great name*, which was profaned among

---

[64]"I will say to the north, Give up; and to the south, Keep not back: bring my sons from far, and my daughters from the ends of the earth; Even every one that is called by my name: for I have created him for my glory, I have formed him; yea, I have made him." Isaiah 43:6–7.

[65]Edwards, "End for Which God Created the World" *WJE* 8:479.

[66]Ibid., 494.

the heathen."⁶⁷ Again, God's name was debased before the non-Christian nations. Thus, God guarantees to engage in a missional work—namely, advancing his kingdom in the world. He will visibly act so as to vindicate his name among the nations. God's glory is ultimate in his motives for every action. It was his purpose not only in creating the world, but also in reconciling it back to himself.

Edwards resolves, "It would be endless to enumerate particular places wherein this appears; wherein the saints declare this, by expressing their earnest desires of God's praise; calling on all nations, and all beings in heaven and earth to praise him."⁶⁸ Again, Edwards points the reader's attention to the transnational scope of God's creative purposes by saying that "all nations" are called upon to praise God. This calling upon the nations to praise him is missional language in that it is a call to advance the kingdom of Christ on earth.

Summary

Central to our idea of a missional reading is that Edwards brings his theological points out in the context of a transnational spreading of the gospel. The idea is that the kingdom of God would advance into non-Christian arenas through the communication of God's glory. This communicative act is not a desire to fill something that is lacking from within, but it is an overflow of God's perfections within himself. Out of his own good pleasure, God's intra-Trinitarian love overflows outside of himself and to his creatures. All of human history is set within God's sovereign will and redemptive purposes. Moreover, it is moving towards a determined and certain end. Edwards's *End for Which God Created the World* demonstrates a clear theology of mission in that it promotes God's sovereignty as its source and foundation. God's sovereign goal for all of human history is to glorify himself in the creature's delight of himself. This goal will be brought about in all nations by God's sovereign will and power. Inevitably, the non-Christian nations will gradually come to a saving knowledge of God's glory. This ultimate end will come about by the church's promulgation the gospel in foreign lands. The nations will be converted, societies will be transformed, and God will be glorified.

---

[67] Ibid. Italics original.

[68] Ibid, 501.

Chapter 2

The Universal Depravity of Humankind

THE ULTIMATE FOUNDATION of all of Edwards's theology of mission is a belief in the sovereignty of God. In the previous chapter, our focus was on God's authority and sovereign will to do what he pleases, which includes the salvation of the unbeliever living outside of Christendom. In this chapter, the attention shifts towards humankind's depravity and need of forgiveness. Originally created good and perfect, humankind was made in the image and likeness of God. Yet, due to the rebellion of Adam and Even in the garden, humankind was cursed for their transgression. Humans are now affected with the stain of a divine curse which separates them from God. They stand condemned and guilty before a holy God. As a result of this divine curse, there is a fundamental change of human nature. Humans now have an inherited guilt and a sinful nature. Their personal sins are an evidence of that sinful nature, yet Edwards held to a traditionally Reformed positon.[1] This doctrine maintains humankind guilt is due not only because of the sins they actually commit, but also due to their participation with Adam and Eve's sin in the garden.[2] Consequently, humans today have an

---

[1] In his treatise *Freedom of the Will*, Edwards he aligns himself with the Reformed tradition and criticizes the Arminian teaching of human depravity. He writes in his conclusion a summary of his main objections, "The things which have been said, obviate some of the chief objections of Arminians against the Calvinistic doctrine of the total depravity and corruption of man's nature, whereby his heart is wholly under the power of sin, and he is utterly unable, without the interposition of sovereign grace, savingly to love God, believe in Christ, or do anything that is truly good and acceptable in God's sight." Jonathan Edwards, *Freedom of the Will*, ed. Paul Ramsey, vol. 1 of *The Works of Jonathan Edwards* [WJE] (New Haven: Yale, 1970), 432. Italics original.

[2] Edwards writes, "Both guilt, or exposedness to punishment, and also depravity of heart, came upon Adam's posterity just as they came upon him, as much as if he and they had all coexisted,

inherited guilt from birth, and therefore, they stand condemned and in need of God's forgiveness.

For Edwards, the depravity of humanity is presented as the need of salvation. Casting the doctrine in these terms creates the need for world mission. "The great salvation by Christ stands in direct relation to this ruin, as the remedy to the disease; and the whole gospel, or doctrine of salvation, must suppose it; and all real belief, or true notion of that gospel, must be built upon it."[3] The entire human race stands condemned and in need of salvation. Edwards's analysis of this brokenness sees the beginning of world mission. Our argument in this chapter is to show that when Edwards spoke of human depravity, he often cast it in missional terms.

As per our proposed format, we will begin our survey with a historical-theological analysis of Edwards's doctrine of universal human depravity insofar as it intersects with the theme of world mission. This analysis will focus on three key areas. Taken together, they develop a picture of Edwards's theology of mission. First, Edwards often speaks of human depravity as equally affecting everyone, regardless of their background. His point is that the consequences of sin are common to every person. Furthermore, in order for salvation to be wrought in the world, humankind must receive revelation from God.[4] This global need for human salvation stresses the *universality* of the need for world mission. Second, Edwards presents God as holy and righteous. Since God is holy and righteous, the nations are to be judged for their sin—namely, their idolatry and wickedness. Yet, for a select group of people coming from every tongue, tribe, and nation, God will extend his staying hand of mercy. This aspect of Edwards's theology creates a supreme *priority* in world mission—God's vindicating his own

---

like a tree with many branches; allowing only for the difference necessarily resulting from the place Adam stood in, as head or root of the whole, and being first and most immediately dealt with, and most immediately acting and suffering. Otherwise, it is as if, in every step of proceeding, every alteration in the root had been attended, at the same instant, with the same steps and alterations throughout the whole tree, in each individual branch. I think, this will naturally follow on the supposition of there being a constituted oneness or identity of Adam and his posterity in this affair." Thus, Edwards says that Adam and his posterity share in the guilt of sin. In some sense, Adam's future generations took part in his sin in the garden. Therefore, they stand in equal condemnation for that sin. Jonathan Edwards, *Original Sin*, ed. Clyde A. Holbrook, vol. 3 of *The Works of Jonathan Edwards* [*WJE*] (New Haven: Yale University Press, 1970), 389–90. Italics original.

[3] Edwards, *Original Sin, WJE* 3:103.

[4] Here, we mean that God dispenses his special revelation through the church preaching the gospel. This point will be made clearer in chapter five when the promulgation of the gospel is shown to be the proper method of world mission.

name. Third, Edwards's creative doctrine of the *prisca theologia* displays a hopeful optimism underpinning human depravity. This teaching creates a confident *expectation* for the global success of world mission.

Finally, we will present a missional reading of Edwards's treatise *Original Sin*. This work is our representative text that will show Edwards's hamartiology intersecting at key points with world mission. Again, our task is not to trace the entire argument of this treatise. Our aim is to draw out key themes of the treatise as it relates to the advancement of the kingdom of God on earth.

The Need for a Theology of Mission: A Historical-Theological Survey

Equal Condemnation for All

Whenever discussing the doctrine of human depravity, Edwards often spoke of the universality of its scope. All are guilty of sin. Edwards writes, "The Scriptures are so very express in it, that all mankind, *all flesh, all the world,* every man living, are guilty of sin."[5] There is not one human, institution, tradition, or culture that remains unaffected by the corruption of sin. Every race, ethnicity, and nationality is under the curse of the Fall. Yet, Edwards held that all human beings have intrinsic value as they are created in the image and likeness of God. With direct implications for the Mohawk and Housatonic Indians, George Marsden writes, "[I]f Edwards had a dim view of the natives' culture, he believed their faults arose not out of any inherent inferiority, but from being part of the human race."[6] Both the Native Americans and the British colonialists are equally fallen and in need of divine forgiveness. There is no innate superiority or inferiority based on race, ethnicity, or background. The British colonials and the Native Americans were equally in a fallen condition. Simply because Edwards believed his fellow countrymen were part of a politer and more refined society, they were just as lost and in need of God's saving mercies. In short, all who are unconverted stand condemned before God because of their sinful nature.

Edwards did not believe that any race had an innate superiority. Surely, he held that the culture and traditions of the British was higher and prefer-

---

[5] Edwards, *Original Sin, WJE* 3:134. Italics original.
[6] George Marsden, *Jonathan Edwards: A Life,* 442.

able due to centuries of Christian influence.[7] However, Edwards viewed those within Christendom under an even greater judgment due to their privileged position. To be within the blessings of Christian society was a benefit that should not be squandered. If a person did not make use of the benefits of living in a Christian society, they would be guilty of forsaking an opportunity not all are afforded. "[H]e believed most of the Europeans in North America were equally degenerate, but worse for having rejected so many opportunities to hear the Gospel."[8] They would be willfully rejecting Christianity, whereas the unbeliever—who had no opportunity to accept or reject the benefits of Christendom—would not. To Edwards, the average British subject who was baptized into the faith and raised with gospel truth, yet was coldhearted to gospel religion, was under an even stricter and severe judgment than of the Indian who had no knowledge of the truths of Scripture. Edwards wrote,

> To what a pass are things come in Protestant countries at this day, and in our nation in particular! To what a prodigious height has a deluge of infidelity, profaneness, luxury, debauchery and wickedness of every kind, arisen! The poor savage Americans are mere babes and fools (if I may so speak) as to proficiency in wickedness, in comparison of multitudes that the Christian world throngs with.[9]

Apart from a communication of the gospel message, the prospects of an eternity in hell is sure–for both the person living under Christendom and the unbeliever. Edwards points to the parable of the Laborers in the Vineyard in Matthew 20:1–16 for support. He writes, "Many in Christendom are called, by the outward call of God's Word, and yet few of them are in a state of salvation: but not all these that sit under the sound of the gospel, and hear its invitations, are fit to come to sacraments."[10] Many Pharisees

---

[7] "Edwards differed little from his contemporaries in his views of Indian culture, and he found in Indian society proof of the truth of Calvinist doctrine against Arminian challenges. When he looked at America's Indian population, he found confirmation of the absolute necessity of regenerating grace." Rachel M. Wheeler, "Edwards as Missionary," in *The Cambridge Companion to Jonathan Edwards*, ed. Stephen J. Stein (Cambridge University Press: New York, 2007), 202.

[8] Ibid.

[9] Edwards, *Original Sin*, WJE 3:183.

[10] Jonathan Edwards, "An Humble Inquiry into the Rules of the Word of God" in *Ecclesiastical Writings*, ed. David. D. Hall, vol. 12 of *The Works of Jonathan Edwards* [WJE] (New Haven: Yale University Press, 1994), 285.

and Sadducees labored hard in the vineyard, expecting a reward "above the gentile converts or proselytes."[11] Not only did they receive no reward, they received condemnation.

Edwards makes this point more explicit in his work *Misrepresentations Corrected, and Truth Vindicated*. He writes,

> I would observe one thing further under this head, viz. that ungodly men which live under the gospel, notwithstanding any moral sincerity they may have, are worse, and more provoking enemies to God, than the very heathen, who never sinned against gospel light and mercy. This is very manifest by the Scriptures, particularly Matt. 10:13–14; Amos 3:2; Rom. 2:9; 2 Pet. 2:21; Rev. 3:15–16.[12]

The person living under the benefits of Christendom is under stricter judgment for his willful neglect or rejection of the gospel in comparison to the unbeliever living outside Christendom.[13] The person who lives outside of Christendom is still under God's wrath, but the condemnation is much worse for those living within its borders. This stricter condemnation is because they have had opportunity to hear the gospel and benefit from its promises whereas the unbeliever living outside Christendom has not been afforded that opportunity.

Thus, all are in need of redemption—those living inside Christendom and those outside. They need salvation revealed to them. Without divine revelation, they are lost forever. "Without a revelation now extant, or once extant, having some remaining influence by tradition, men would undoubtedly forever be at a loss what God expects from us and what we may expect from him."[14] Humankind needs to hear who God is and what is required of them. This need is the universal need of world mission.

---

[11] Ibid.

[12] Edwards, "Misrepresentations Corrected, and Truth Vindicated" in *Ecclesiastical Writings*, WJE 12:420.

[13] Moreover, Edwards says this dereliction of duty to believe the gospel is common for those living in Christendom. He writes, "[One] instance of the natural stupidity of the minds of mankind, that I shall observe, is that great disregard of their own eternal interest; which appears so remarkably, so generally, among them that live under the gospel." Edwards, *Original Sin*, WJE 3:152.

[14] Jonathan Edwards, "Miscellanies no. 1338" *WJE* 23:347.

Divine Victory Over the Nations

Now that we have established the universality of Edwards's need for world mission, we must now identify its priority. God is holy and stands as the righteous judge over the nations. Humankind is guilty and a just recompense is due. We will see from the following analysis that Edwards placed God's vindicating his name above all other things as the supreme priority in world mission. This vindication is simultaneously realized in God's judgment on the nations and in his saving mercy on a select group from the nations—namely, his elect.

God's judgment of the nations is deserved due to their wickedness and idolatry. They do not fear God. Worthless idols are set up for worship. Thus, God acts to restore his name by publically triumphing over the nations (and their idols). He does this in order to manifest his superiority to them. Evaluating the grand scope of redemptive history, Edwards preaches a sermon on Genesis 10:10–12. In this narrative, Abraham experiences victory over unbelieving kings in battle. Edwards points to a typological foreshadowing seen in Abraham's conquest. He writes, "This he received of God as a pledge of what he had promised, viz. the victory that Christ his seed should obtain over all nations of the earth whereby he should possess the gate of his enemies. 'Tis plainly spoken of as such in the forty-first chapter of Isaiah. In that chapter is foretold the future glorious victory the church shall obtain over the nations of the world."[15] Linking these texts shows Edwards's creative intertextuality at work. Edwards saw the Abrahamic conquest as a type of victory Christ would have over rebellious non-Christian nations.[16] Inevitably, God would rise up to vindicate his name among the nations by striking down all his enemies. His kingdom would advance throughout the world by a progress of the Christian religion. Moreover, this progress was done by preaching the gospel to the nations. They would repent of their idolatry and accept the gospel message.

Edwards further illustrates this point in an extended reflection in one of his "Miscellanies" entitled "Christian Religion. Fulfillment of the Prophecies of Messiah in the Conversion of the Gentiles from Heathenism by the Means of Jesus." Edwards writes, "So God is represented in the prophecies of Isaiah as gloriously manifesting himself as above the gods of the heathen, in appear-

---

[15] Jonathan Edwards, *A History of the Work of Redemption*, WJE 9:162–163.

[16] See David Barshinger, "'The Only Rule of Our Faith and Practice': Jonathan Edwards's Interpretation of the Book of Isaiah as a Case Study of His Exegetical Boundaries," *Journal of the Evangelical Theological Society*, hereafter JETS 52:4 (2009): 812.

ing above Bel and Nebo, the idols of Babylon, when Babylon was destroyed and the Jews delivered from their captivity there."[17] This triumphing over the non-Christian nations and gods demonstrates a missional impetus. The advancement of the Christian religion happens by God's conquering over all rivals. Edwards continues by connecting this to the success of the Christian gospel. "But the Babylonish Empire was but a small thing in comparison of the Roman Empire, which Christ converted from heathenism."[18]

Further, Edwards saw an order and process to God's redemptive work. "This being the method God takes with the world, first to make a revelation of his dreadful majesty and justice before he reveals his grace."[19] Not only is a corporate or national element in view, Edwards sees a possible connection to how God individually deals with persons. He writes, "[S]o 'tis but reasonable to suppose that this is his common method with particular persons, first to awaken them to a sense of the dreadful justice of God and his displeasure against sin, and then to give them a sense of his grace."[20] While there was judgment due to sin and rebellion, there would be mercy and salvation due to God's grace. God pronounces judgment in order to maintain the standard of his holiness. Sins against his law will not be tolerated and divine judgment is pronounced. Combined with his reflections on theological anthropology, Edwards's view of divine judgment creates a need for world mission. Necessary for mission to take place, people must be redeemed from something. In other words, if humankind is not sinful and in a fallen condition, there is no need for redemption. Yet, they are tainted with the guilt of sin and rebellion. The nations are lost and without hope—-in need of a saving work from God. While Edwards's doctrine of sin presents a bleak forecast on mankind's plight, his outlook is ultimately one of eschatological hope for the nations.

As the days neared closer to the future promises, God would shine his light into darkness. The non-Christian nations and unregenerate would incur divine judgment, and the entire world would come under the direct care and blessing of the Lord. This period of divine favor—-namely, the millennial reign of Christ spoken of in Revelation 20–would be a future golden age of earthly prosperity. This period marks the culmination of God's victory over idolatry and wickedness. The nations would abandon their

---

[17] Edwards, "Miscellanies no. 1327" *WJE* 23:308.

[18] Ibid.

[19] Edwards, "Miscellanies no. 337" *WJE* 13:412.

[20] Ibid.

false religions and come to a knowledge of the glory of the Lord. Since the depravity of man is universal in its scope, God's judgment and his blessing would be likewise universal in its scope. The extent of the millennium, for Edwards, was worldwide—not limited to one nationality or ethnic group. In the near future, the promised millennium would be realized, and all peoples would be sanctified.[21] Edwards saw an unequivocal universality to the thousand years. Not simply limited to the civilized culture of the European world, all peoples of the earth would experience the providential care and watch of God. This type of blessing included, but was not limited to, political peace, economic prosperity, international stability and harmony, ecclesiastical strength, and the flourishing of genuine piety of the individual Christian. Drawing on prophecy found in Isaiah 32:3–4, Edwards envisions a future day:

> And then all countries and nations, even those that are now most ignorant, shall be full of light and knowledge. Great knowledge shall prevail everywhere. It may be hoped that then many of the Negroes and Indians will be divines, and that excellent books will be published in Africa, in Ethiopia, in Turkey—and not only very learned men, but others that are more ordinary men, shall then be very knowing in religion.[22]

Yet, this progress in Christian scholarship would not simply be the non-Christian nations being brought to the level of civilized nations. All people would be blessed in unimaginable ways. Edwards laments in one of his "Miscellanies" on the millennium that the present age struggles in its incomplete understanding of God's Word. The church has not fully plumbed the depths of Scripture, as there are obscure portions the most skilled scholars still cannot properly interpret. There are many things left to be further studied. Yet, the church will come to discover new truths about God through it in the future.

> How happy will that state be, when neither divine nor human learning shall be confined and imprisoned within only two or three nations of Europe, but shall be diffused all over the world,

---

[21] Edwards's view on the nearness of the millennium is of some scholarly debate. This statement is not meant to imply a particular position in that discussion. See Brandon G. Withrow, "A Future of Hope: Jonathan Edwards and Millennial Expectations," *Trinity Journal* 22 (2001): 75–98.

[22] Edwards, *A History of the Work of Redemption*, WJE 9:480.

and this lower world shall be all over covered with light, the various parts of it mutually enlightening each other; when the most barbarous nations shall become as bright and polite as England; when ignorant heathen lands shall be stocked with most profound divines and most learned philosophers; when we shall from time to time have the most excellent books and wonderful performances brought from one end of the earth and another to surprise us—sometimes new and wondrous discoveries from Terra Australis Incognita, admirable books of devotion, the most divine and angelic strains from among the Hottentots, and the press shall groan in wild Tartary.[23]

This vision of mutual enlightening is a brief picture of what the millennium will bring to the world. Nations who were formerly non-Christian are now seen as enlightening areas that are now considered Christendom. The glory of God has covered the earth to the extent that formerly non-Christian nations are now at the vanguard of theological and philosophical discoveries. For Edwards, the thought of this future glory is ineffable. Edwards goes on to write, "The distant extremes of the world shall shake hands together and all nations shall be acquainted, and they shall all join the forces of their minds in exploring the glories of the Creator, their hearts in loving and adoring him, their hands in serving him, and their voices in making the world to ring with his praise."[24]

Edwards states the place of world missions in the hastening of the millennial reign of Christ. He writes, "Another end of thus keeping his church in hope, is to quicken and enliven their endeavors to propagate religion and to advance the kingdom of Jesus."[25] The Christian faith will see great advancements and will ultimately prevail over false religions through the propagation of the gospel. Edwards says that it is probable that the gospel will be met with opposition.[26] Yet, as the truth of the gospel increases throughout the world, its glory is displayed and vindicated. This is a promised future, and it is meant to encourage both Christian magistrates and ministers alike. This assurance of success in gospel advancement is

---

[23] Edwards, "Miscellanies no. 26" *WJE* 13:212.

[24] Ibid., 213.

[25] Edwards, "Miscellanies no. 351" *WJE* 13:426.

[26] Ibid., 429.

meant to strengthen the hope and resolve of the church, that they would continue on with the duties of religion with greater boldness and joy.

Edwards predicts that there will be "a vastly more glorious propagation of the true religion before the end of the world."[27] Edwards makes reference to the stronghold Satan has over the world. He goes on in this same passage to compare the Egyptian magicians' deceptive powers with that of Islam's stronghold over certain nations. In a contest of powers, Christ will progressively prevail over Satan, advancing his kingdom throughout the world via the evangelist's message. He continues the metaphor, comparing this advancement with Moses's victory over the magicians. Here, Edwards emphasizes the power of the gospel. He writes, "The propagation of the Christian church is often spoken of in Scripture as a glorious instance of the conquering power of God and Christ; and therefore, without doubt, it shall be carried far as to be vastly beyond what Satan has done to vie with Christ."[28] Thus, the task of missions has a prominent place in the events immediately preceding the millennium. Again, the priority of God is shown in his "conquering power." He is shown having victory over the nations, publically displaying his power and authority over false gods.

Edwards envisioned a day in the millennium when all would experience ineffable glories of spiritual energy and vitality. He contrasts the thousand years with the current religious climate, "Religion shall not be an empty profession as it now mostly is, but holiness of heart and life shall abundantly prevail."[29] It will be a time like no other. Political leaders will uphold righteousness and do justice. Clergy will lead Christ's church in a worthy manner. Quoting Daniel 2:34 where a stone will break the image's feet of iron and clay, Edwards opines, "One nation shall be enlightened and converted after another, one false religion and false way of worship exploded after another."[30] During the millennium, the influence of false religions will greatly diminish, and the impact of true religion will grow and intensify. Again, this is explicitly missional language.

But before moving on, we will reflect on the priority of world mission. God's name being vindicated in the nations is the supreme priority for God

---

[27] Jonathan Edwards, "Miscellanies no. 613" in *The "Miscellanies": (Entry Nos. 501–832)*, ed. Ava Chamberlain, vol. 18 of *The Works of Jonathan Edwards* [*WJE*] (New Haven: Yale University Press, 2000), 145.

[28] Ibid., 146.

[29] Edwards, *A History of the Work of Redemption, WJE* 9:481.

[30] Ibid., 459.

in world mission. The idolatry and wickedness of the nations has moved God to restore his honor. The Gentile nations stand condemned before a holy God. He has promised to execute judgment on them by triumphing over them. Yet, for a remnant, God will show mercy, and he will save them. But how might this happen? In our next section, we will examine Edwards's doctrine of the *prisca theologia*. This teaching shows the manner in which God has prepared the world for the success of the gospel.

A Catalyzing Agent for Mission

One underappreciated element of Edwards's theology is the doctrine of the *prisca theologia*.[31] Edwards developed this teaching in order to provide a missional underpinning to sin's effects on the world. Briefly stated, mankind is under a curse where the entire person is effected by their sin. Moreover, human civilizations and cultures are also effected. The music, language, art, history, philosophy and traditions human culture develops are all polluted with the stain of sin. Yet, in spite of a broken nature, vestiges of God's redemptive purposes are revealed in culture and traditions.[32]

Gerald McDermott was the first to connect Edwards with the concept of *prisca theologia* in his book *Jonathan Edwards Confronts the Gods*.[33] Broadly defined, this teaching sees non-Christian traditions paralleling and complementing Christian doctrine. These traditions are incomplete and distorted beyond proper recognition divorced from further revelation. Edwards calls these vestiges "scraps of truth."[34] This corresponding structure exists because all cultures around the globe, regardless of race or religion, derive from a singular point in human history. At one point in primeval history, Christian truth was known and preached to the entire human race. Thus, every human culture derives its being and practices from an earlier point where God was known in truth. This divine truth was not communicated

---

[31] *Prisca theologia* is a Latin term meaning: "ancient theology."

[32] C.f. Amy Plantinga Pauw, *The Supreme Harmony of All: The Trinitarian Theology of Jonathan Edwards* (Grand Rapids: Eerdmans, 2002), Kindle.

[33] Gerald McDermott, *Jonathan Edwards Confronts the Gods: Christian Theology, Enlightenment Religion, and Non-Christian Faiths* (New York: Oxford University Press, 2000).

[34] This phrase comes in a comment on Acts 17:26–27. He says that God made a way for mankind to genuinely seek after him if they so desired. "[God] scattered abroad upon the face of the earth, that provision should be made in providence at all times, that the nations of the world, if their heart had been well disposed to seek after the truth, might have had some means to have led 'em in their sincere and diligent inquiries to the knowledge of the true God and his ways." Edwards, *Notes on Scripture*, WJE 15:370.

in its fully realized form, but only in an embryonic shape. It could be that the Noah's good sons or some other antediluvian person was the source of that knowledge. Just like the child's game telephone, where one passes a secret down the line, it is most likely that the original message is corrupted, yet it has some semblance of the original idea. When the game is completed and the truth is revealed in light of the distorted message, the differences can be clearly seen. At the end, everyone is able look back and compare the distorted reality from the truth.

McDermott sees Edwards as being greatly intrigued with this teaching, and developing it to his own theological context.[35] He writes,

> Edwards was clearly impressed by these proponents of the *prisca theologia*. He copied enormous extracts from their works into his private notebooks. Yet, as Diderot once said, imitation is continual invention. From his marginal notes and recapitulation of the tradition in other private notebooks, it is clear that Edwards was selectively refashioning the tradition to serve his own polemical needs. His principal purpose was to show, against the deists, that nearly all humans have received revelation, and therefore all knowledge of true religion among the heathen is from revelation rather than the light of natural reason.[36]

Edwards's purpose in using this teaching was to combat the Deists' argument that people living outside of Christendom have acquired true knowledge about God apart from divine revelation. They asserted that human reason, unassisted by divine intervention, could attain to true spiritual knowledge. Edwards rejected this argument. If the person living outside of Christendom knew accurate truths about God, it was only because they received it from revelation.[37] The person might have heard from Jewish sources. Edwards writes, "Heathen had what they had of truth in divine things by tradition from the first fathers of nations, or from the Jews."[38] In another place, he

---

[35] See Michael McClymond and Gerald McDermott, *The Theology of Jonathan Edwards* (New York: Oxford University Press, 2012), 580–8, 596–7.

[36] McDermott, *Jonathan Edwards Confronts the Gods*, 94.

[37] They may have received the information from someone who was accurately communicating Scriptural truth. Whatever the case, the unbeliever did not come to that conclusion through pure and unassisted human reason alone. For Edwards, the source is always divine revelation.

[38] Jonathan Edwards, "Miscellanies no. 959" in *The "Miscellanies": (Entry Nos. 833–1152)*, ed. Amy Plantinga Pauw, vol. 20 of *The Works of Jonathan Edwards* [WJE] (New Haven: Yale University Press, 2000), 239.

similarly writes, "That the heathen philosophers had their notions of the unity of God, of the Trinity, of the immortality of the soul, the last judgment, the general conflagration, etc. by tradition, from the first ages of the world and from the Jewish nation, is manifest by their own testimony."[39] In one place, Edwards goes so far as to say that any knowledge that is profitable and good—not just limited to spiritual truths—came from divine revelation. He writes, "Human learning and all useful and noble knowledge, and not only knowledge in things divine and spiritual, was originally from the church of God in all ages of the world, ... so that [no] barbarous nation has received so much as civility, but from the church of Christ."[40] He used the tradition of the *prisca theologia* to uphold the teaching that divine revelation was essential for gaining true spiritual knowledge about God.[41] Our argument in this section is to further this claim by observing how Edwards connects it to the theme of world mission.

Jews were a source of this divine revelation. Yet, God could also immediately impart these "scraps of truth." In one particular entry, Edwards says that divine inspiration was not limited to the nation of Israel.[42] He points to Balaam's prophecy as evidence of this theory. He also notes dreams given by God to unbelievers outside of God's people. He says that the wise men who came from the east were under divine inspiration when they received word to visit the infant Jesus. Additionally, he looks to the Exodus narrative. He says that Pharaoh, the cup bearer, and the baker were subjects of revelatory dreams, all of a divine origin. He also says Nebuchadnezzar, although a wicked and idolatrous ruler, received visions that prepared the way for God to act. Looking outside Scripture, Edwards says that non-Christian philosophers such as Socrates and Plato may have been subjects of direct inspiration of God. Edwards's point is not to say that this revelation was of a salvific nature. The revelation was given that "they might dispose the heathen nations, as they had occasion to converse with the Jews and to be informed of the revelations and prophecies that they had among them, to attend the more to them and to inquire into them and their evidences."[43]

---

[39] Edwards, "Miscellanies no. 953" *WJE* 20:222.

[40] Edwards, "Miscellanies no. 962" *WJE* 20:245.

[41] McDermott notes how Edwards particularly looked to theologians such a Theophilus Gale (1628–1678), Chevalier Ramsay (1686–1743), and Philip Skelton (1707–1787) for insights into this tradition. McDermott, *Jonathan Edwards Confronts the Gods*, 92.

[42] Edwards, "Miscellanies no. 1162" *WJE* 23:84–5.

[43] Ibid., 85.

When they receive the revelation, they are to press deeper into its meaning and inquire as to its origin. The hope is that they might find the true source of its basis—namely, God. These vestiges of truth are meant to be signposts that point the observer to back God. In other words, they are missional in nature.

Certain truths revealed to them through their analysis of reason, tradition, providence, nature, logic, etc., could be a way that God has made them ready to accept the gospel whenever it does arrive. So, when these people come into direct contact with the gospel, they would be more likely to accept the things of God because they have been divinely prepared for it. Edwards writes, "[These revelations] might prepare the Gentile nations ... to receive the gospel when God's time came for its promulgation among these nations, by disposing them the more diligently and impartially to attend to it."[44] The reason for such revelation given to the philosophers was so that these people could better understand the gospel when it arrived. It would also give them a sense of God's beauty and excellency when they fully understood both the gospel and the means by which God revealed himself in the preparatory work.

Moreover, Edwards believed these revelatory acts would confirm the truthfulness of the Christian religion. "Things that appeared in the heathen world before, in and after Christ's time that have reference to him, that confirm the Christian religion."[45] Thus, they had an apologetic effect. There were signs before, during, and after the time of Christ that point the nations to God. For example, Edwards notes the Roman historians, Suetonius and Tacitus, recorded that many eastern nations expected a person would arise out of Judea who would govern the whole world.[46] He proceeds to give other numerous examples where those located outside God's chosen people acknowledge something that attest to the beauty and excellency of God. The eclipse of the sun at Christ's passion was also a sign to the nations. All these signs would go towards verifying the authenticity of the message, thus, enlightening the subjects, making them ready for gospel proclamation.

To summarize this teaching of the *prisca theologia*, Edwards's view of the fall of mankind was coupled with a preparatory aspect of conversion. This idea directly implied an embedded theology of mission. Although the image of God was distorted in the Fall, humankind is not left without hope. There

---

[44] Ibid.

[45] Edwards, "Miscellanies no. 981" *WJE* 20:299.

[46] Ibid., 299–302.

are vestigial traces of the gospel entrenched into the fabric of every human society. Without the light of illumination, these traces are unable to be fully and properly discerned. However, when the true gospel is preached in these lands, the people will be able to quickly and easily see what has been there all along—-God's truth hidden in plain sight. In other words, Edwards held a strongly Reformed teaching of total depravity, yet simultaneously he held to an innovative view which saw people who were totally depraved as being prepared for gospel proclamation. There are vestiges of the gospel scattered throughout the world which are intended to ignite revival. The non-Christian nations which are currently blinded to the truth of the gospel would have an unmasking. Therefore, Edwards's teaching on the subject of humanity and sin were laced with missional elements.

Original Sin: A Missional Reading

In this section, we will take Edwards's treatise *Original Sin* as the representative work for his doctrine of the universal depravity of man. It provides the clearest expression of the global need for mission. This treatise is a work of constructive theology which seeks to show that all people have sinned and stand condemned before God.[47] This position stands in contrast to the progressive spirit of the eighteenth century optimism of the Enlightenment. "The emphasis on human freedom and innate capacities for virtue reflected growing modern tendencies toward views that men, or at least gentlemen, could control their own destinies."[48] As is a typical approach of Edwards, he stands firm within the Reformed tradition, yet presents it in a creative and winsome way. This approach is seen particularly in his emphasis on the equality of all persons, regardless of their race, ethnicity or background. Edwards saw all people as bearing the image and likeness of God. There is no innate superiority in one person or people group over another. Thus, Edwards's treatise was written in large part to establish a global need for redemption.

Finished the last year of his life, Edwards wrote *The Great Christian Doctrine of Original Sin Defended* partially in response to the work of the

---

[47] Surely, the treatise was written as a polemic, but the totality of Edwards's work should not be seen as merely a refutation of John Taylor's work. Edwards wrote in the opening line to the preface, "The following discourse is intended, not merely as an answer to any particular book written against the doctrine of original sin, but as a general defense of that great important doctrine." Edwards, *Original Sin*, WJE 3:102.

[48] Marsden, *Jonathan Edwards: A Life,* 451.

English theologian John Taylor (1694–1761). Taylor argued strongly against the Reformed understanding of the doctrine of Original Sin in his 1740 work entitled *The Scripture-Doctrine of Original Sin, Proposed to Free and Candid Examination*. In this work, Taylor sought to examine Scripture and present a case against the Calvinist position. His work was so influential that some ministers were turning from the Reformed view.[49] In Edwards's response, he sought to not only dismantle Taylor's work, but also present a rational and biblical case for the traditionally Reformed teaching.

The Universal Tendency to Sin

One of the foundational components of this treatise is Edwards's stress on the universality of humankind's depravity. In discussing the worldwide of scope depravity, he writes,

> In God's sight no man living can be justified; but all are sinners, and exposed to condemnation. This is true of persons of all constitutions, capacities, conditions, manners, opinions and educations; in all countries, climates, nations and ages; and through all the mighty changes and revolutions, which have come to pass in the habitable world.[50]

There is no coincidence in how Edwards presents this doctrine in such wide-ranging language. From the highest ranking member of polite British society to the lowest member of the non-Christian tribe, all are sinners and stand condemned before God. Sin transcends race, nationality, ethnicity, personality, age, and cultural or historical setting. Making various practical observations about the effects of sin on the human race, Edwards's treatise seeks to answer how to give an account for every human's tendency to sin. Does it derive from an innate free choice–uninhibited from external effects on the will? Or is a consequence of every person's innate corruption?

Edwards claims that sin is not due to one's circumstances, but due to one's very nature. It is not as though the surrounding external conditions determine a person's behavior. But it is the person's inward condition that produces their behavior. Further, everything in the world is stained by the

---

[49] "Charles Chauncy, for one, was inspired by Taylor's volumes to spend seven years after the awakening revising his doctrines away from his earlier Calvinism." Marsden, *Jonathan Edwards: A Life,* 436.

[50] Edwards, *Original Sin, WJE* 3:102.

touch of sin. There is nothing outside its influence. Edwards writes, "The universality of the effect [of sin] shews that the cause was universal, and not anything belonging to the particular circumstances of one, or only some nations or ages, but something belonging to that nature that is common to all nations, and that remains the same through all ages."[51]

This reality is confirmed that all humans, regardless of their circumstances choose sin. Edwards comments on this observation, "Because they are observed in mankind in general, through all countries, nations and ages, and in all conditions."[52] The choice to sin is not constrained by outward forces, such as one's traditions or culture, but it is chosen freely. This free choice always chooses sin because it is an outflow of a corrupted nature. This nature is embedded deep in every single human heart. Edwards writes,

> How comes it to pass, that the free will of mankind has been determined to evil, in like manner before the flood, and after the flood; under the law, and under the gospel; among both Jews and Gentiles, under the Old Testament; and since that, among Christians, Jews, Mohametans; among Papists and Protestants; in those nations where civility, politeness, arts and learning most prevail, and among the Negroes and Hottentots in Africa, the Tartars in Asia, and Indians in America, towards both the poles, and on every side of the globe; in greatest cities, and obscurest villages; in palaces, and in huts, wigwams and cells under ground?[53]

Again, Edwards articulates his position with a global awareness. He says that the person living within Christendom is under a greater weight of condemnation. Edwards expresses the doctrine of human depravity in such a way as to highlight the different backgrounds, ethnicities, nationalities, ages, and contexts of persons.

This presentation is made more apparent when one considers the historical setting in which Edwards wrote his treatise. Edwards composed this work while he was daily ministering to the Native Americans at the missionary outpost in Stockbridge. He would have been keenly aware of anthropological disparities in the world as he saw them played out in everyday life. Rachel Wheeler writes, "Had it not been for his mission experience,

---

[51] Ibid., 148.

[52] Ibid., 125.

[53] Ibid., 194.

Edwards might not have emphasized in *Original Sin* the equality in human depravity to the extent that he did."[54] In other words, Edwards's treatise is greatly influenced by his lived experience in cross-cultural ministry. He emphasizes universality of sin's devastating effect on the entire world.

Sin's global effect produces a need for redemption. In other words, this worldwide need is the basis for global missions. In a direct argument against Taylor, Edwards maintains that all humans are faced with a moral inability to choose God. Even if the non-Christian nations "had sufficient light afforded, to know God, and to know and do their whole duty to him; then their inability to deliver themselves must be a moral inability, consisting in a desperate depravity, and most evil disposition of heart."[55] Taylor's argument is that the non-Christian nations are guilty of idolatry. This gross sin is without excuse. Yet, every person has sufficient light to turn to God. Moreover, there exists in every person a libertarian free will that allows them to unreservedly choose to follow God. Conversely, Edwards argues that if that were the case, why has every person decided to choose against God? Surely, it is evident that people choose according to their own carnal desires because of an innate moral corruption. The evidence from human history is unmistakable. Edwards asks rhetorically why it is that throughout all the world—-and all human history—have people freely preferred the same thing?

> How was it with that multitude of nations inhabiting South and North America? What appearance was there, when the Europeans first came hither, of their being recovered, or recovering, in any degree from the grossest ignorance, delusions, and most stupid paganism? And how is it at this day, in those parts of Africa and Asia, into which the light of the gospel has not penetrated?[56]

Again, Edwards's global awareness is evident. His indication of nations all over the world reveals a need for worldwide redemption.

---

[54] Wheeler, "Edwards as Missionary," 206.

[55] Edwards, *Original Sin*, WJE 3:151.

[56] Ibid.

A Missional Recapitulation of Israel's History

God is not simply content to expose the nations to their sinfulness, he also works to reveal himself to the non-Christian nations. In spite of their stubbornness in sin, God's desire to show power and mercy is manifest throughout the entirety of the Scriptures. Edwards's section 8, entitled "The Native Depravity of Mankind Appears, In That There Has Been So Little Good Effect of So Manifold and Great Means, Used to Promote Virtue in the World," is a direct argument against specific points in Taylor's treatise. In this section, Edwards recapitulates the entire biblical narrative with an eye towards missional engagement. This section is the clearest and best example of Edwards's missional theology of universal depravity.

Edwards's purpose in this section is to show the innate sinfulness of mankind notwithstanding the many efforts taken to advance the Christian religion in their midst. Edwards agrees with Taylor's assertion, "The Jewish dispensation had respect to the nations of the world, to spread the knowledge and obedience of God in the earth; and was established for the benefit of all mankind."[57] Edwards affirms that all of the Old Testament events took place so that God might manifest himself to the nations. God's desire is to vindicate his name and spread his glory throughout all the earth. Beginning with Abraham, God took this unbelieving man who was a "person noted in all the principal nations that were then in the world" and used his fame to grab the world's attention.[58] This working to get the non-Christian nations to take notice of God's powerful work is a missional strategy. Furthermore, Edwards highlights two other events in Abraham's life: the rescue of Lot from non-Christian nations and the blessing of Abraham by Melchizedek. In each case, the nations were made aware of God's presence and power. Edwards comments, "God made his [own] name famous by his wonderful distinguishing dispensations towards [Abraham]."[59] Here, we see God's supreme priority as vindicating his name in the nations. His purpose in delivering and prospering Abraham was ultimately to communicate the knowledge of God to the non-Christian nations. Edwards explicitly states this idea, "One would think, [these acts] should have been sufficient to have awakened the attention and consideration of all the nations in that part of

---

[57] Ibid., 172.

[58] Ibid.

[59] Ibid.

the world, and to have led them to the knowledge and worship of the only true God."[60] Unfortunately, they did not come to accept that knowledge.

Edwards continues the narrative, commenting on the destruction of Sodom. This event was evidence to the nations of God's power. He also recounts the stories of Jacob and Joseph. He says that God continued on the same missional pattern. "Great things were done in the sight of the nations of the world, tending to awaken them, and lead them to the knowledge and obedience of the true God."[61] When Joseph was placed in command, he saved "as it were the whole world" from perishing from famine.[62] In acting in this way, Joseph was a type of savior to whom the nations would turn to for deliverance.[63]

Edwards moves on to the narratives of Moses and Joshua. God worked miraculous signs and wonders to display his power to the most prominent non-Christian nation in the world—Egypt. This divine manifestation was so done on such a public stage so that the entire world would be made aware of God's supreme authority. Edwards says these things were done "to convince the nations of the world of the vanity of their false gods, shewing Jehovah to be infinitely above them, in the thing wherein they dealt most proudly, and exhibiting God's awful displeasure at the wickedness of the heathen world."[64]

In the time of the Judges, God "very publicly manifest himself to the nations of the world."[65] Edwards points to Gideon's victory over Gentile nations as evidence. Then, Edwards moves on the period of Israelite kings. "God used new, and in some respects much greater means with the heathen world, to bring them to the knowledge and service of the true God, in the days of David and Solomon."[66] David conquered the nations of Palestine, extended the borders of Israel, and brought God's reign to bear in a manner and scope like no other before him. Then, God established Solomon as the wisest of the kings. All the nations of the earth came to him for counsel and insight. These things were done for the specific purpose of communicating

---

[60] Ibid.

[61] Ibid., 173.

[62] Ibid.

[63] Edwards claims that his name meant "Savior of the World."

[64] Edwards, *Original Sin*, WJE 3:173.

[65] Ibid., 173.

[66] Ibid., 174.

God's glory throughout the entire world. Edwards continues on to list numerous occasions of God's working "in the sight of the Gentile nations, very much tending to enlighten, affect and persuade them."[67] By listing so many instances of God and his people interacting with Gentile nations, Edwards makes clear to show that there is a missional purpose throughout the entire Old Testament. Edwards says, "These great things were done, that the nations in far countries might hear of God's great name, and of his outstretched arm; that all the people of the earth might fear him ... that all the people of the earth might know, that the Lord was God, and that there was none else."[68] However, there was no lasting effect made on the nations. In spite of God's working miraculous signs for their good, the nations continued in rebellion.

Finally, Edwards turns to the Babylonian Captivity and return. Although the Exodus event was possibly the greatest demonstration of missional activity, the exile and return to the land of Canaan was in some ways even greater. "When all these [instances of divine activity] proved ineffectual, God took a new method with the heathen world, and used, in some respects, much greater means to convince and reclaim them."[69] Again, the point must not be missed here. The purpose of God's actions has been—-and will continue to be—missional. God desires to woo and entice the non-Christian nations. His actions are motivated by a desire to "reclaim" the sinful nations. Moreover, God's actions are not driven by a desire to bring about the total destruction of the sinner, as if out of harsh anger. The goal is not condemnation, but restoration. When the Jews were taken off into captivity, they were brought into the "head and heart of the heathen world."[70] There, the Jews brought with them the sacred Scriptures and stories of God's working in history. Certain Jews were brought before the king and testified of the ultimate authority of God. Many great signs were performed in their midst that testified to this transcendent reality. Later, Babylon was overthrown, which was a sign that the non-Christian nations were not ultimately in control. God is proven to be sovereign over the affairs of men. This truth is evidenced in the prophet's message that God would judge the them and return his people to their land. Many of the Jews returned to the land, but some remained through the world. This dispersion

---

[67] Ibid.

[68] Ibid.

[69] Ibid., 175.

[70] Ibid.

of God's people all over allowed them to bring the Scriptures with them. Edwards concludes this spreading out (and the entire preceding narratives) was for a missional purpose. "Thus that light, which God had given them, was in the providence of God, carried abroad into all parts of the world; so that now they had far greater advantages, to come to the knowledge of the truth, in matters of religion, if they had been disposed to improve their advantages."[71] God's message of salvation was now being prepared and made available for the non-Christian nations.

Again, a missional reading analyzes a text from the perspective of the worldwide advancement of the kingdom of God. Edwards's reading of the narrative history of Israel in particular is pervasive with its direct references to God's purposes in revealing himself to the non-Christian nations. God manifests himself in great signs and wonders so that all would come to a saving knowledge of him. Yet, on the whole, the nations did not turn to Christ to be saved. They were indignant in their sin. "And as to the Gentile nations, though there was a glorious success of the gospel amongst them, in the apostles' days; yet probably not one in ten of those that had the gospel preached to 'em, embraced it."[72] In sum, the very purpose of God's working in history is to bring about the salvation of the nations. God shows his unrelenting mercy in his numerous displays of acts of deliverance. God's purpose is to redeem a select group of people from the Gentile nations. Thus, when Edwards communicates his doctrine of sin, he does so in a way that is laced with missional implications.

The Success of the Gospel

In one section, Edwards critiques Taylor's denial that Adam is the federal head, or representative, for all his posterity. Edwards refutes Taylor by saying a proper analysis of Genesis 1–3 and Romans 5 necessitates the interpretation that Adam represented the entire human race in his conscious decision to rebel against God. All of humanity is guilty in Adam and they incur a nature that inclines them toward sin. Regardless of ethnic distinction, background, or upbringing, all stand in condemnation. In contrast, Christ stands as the second Adam, the federal representative of the elect. Adam's work brings guilt and death; Christ's work brings liberation and life. In the midst of Edwards's discourse on theological anthropology and hamartiology,

---

[71] Ibid., 176.

[72] Ibid., 183.

Edwards envisions a future day in which the merits of Christ will be applied to all peoples. "And how great the number will be, that shall actually be the subjects of [Christ's merits], or how great a proportion of the whole race, considering the vast success of the gospel, that shall be in that future extraordinary, exempt, and glorious season, often spoken of, none can tell."[73] One day, the nations will turn to Christ and be saved. The gospel will have success as it goes into the world.

Later, Edwards says that the epistle to the Romans highlights two great truths about the grace of God. The first is the "the universal corruption and misery of mankind."[74] Everyone, everywhere has been effected with the stain of Original Sin. Both Jew and Gentile are corrupt and in need of redemption. The second is the "the greatness of the benefits which believers receive, and the greatness of the glory they have hope of."[75] Furthermore, he says, "[Paul] endeavors to shew the greatness and absoluteness of the dependence of all mankind on the *redemption and righteousness of Christ,* for justification and life, that he might magnify and exalt the Redeemer."[76] That purpose is the design of the entire epistle. The Jews boasted in their privileged position "as if their being distinguished from all other nations by that great privilege."[77] Again, we see a global awareness in Edwards's writings. Sin has permeated into all areas and places of human society. Edwards says that Israel is just as lost in their sin because they looked to the works of the Law for their salvation. However, "[They] had no consideration of the law of nature, written in the hearts of the Gentiles, and of all mankind."[78] The Gentiles also had a law. It was written on their heart. Both the Law of Moses and the law of nature condemned them all.

The Universal Need for Salvation

Edwards claims that all people, regardless of if they are Jews or Gentiles, stand in need of forgiveness. This need creates the need for world mission.

---

[73] Ibid., 260.
[74] Ibid., 336.
[75] Ibid.
[76] Ibid. Italics original.
[77] Ibid., 337.
[78] Ibid.

> So that it follows, by our author's scheme, that none of mankind, neither infants, nor adult persons, neither the more nor less vicious, neither Jews nor Gentiles, neither heathens nor Christians, ever did, or ever could stand in any need of a saviour; and that, with respect to all, the truth is, Christ is dead in vain.[79]

The work of Christ's redemption is meant to be sufficient for all. Again, Edwards builds upon the idea that there is a universal depravity of humankind. The guilt of original sin equally applies to all. He goes on to highlight this point,

> That it is a truth of the utmost certainty, with respect to every man, born of the race of Adam, by ordinary generation, that *unless he be born again, he cannot see the kingdom of God.* This is true, not only of the heathen, but of them that are born of the professing people of God, as Nicodemus, and the Jews, and every man born of the flesh.[80]

The totality of the human race is unable to produce within themselves salvation. They must look outside of themselves for salvation. They simply cannot achieve redemption on their own. All stand in need of a savior.

One only need to observe human history to see that all persons are in need of redemption. The fact that all humans are in need of salvation is a point made not only by Scripture, but also evidenced by plain reason. The standard teaching human depravity been taught from since before Pentecost. It was taught by ancient Jewish scholars and Rabbis. Edwards says that even the most learned non-Christian philosophers adopted the teaching because it is consistent with logic and experience. Edwards writes, "As this doctrine of original corruption was constantly maintained in the church of God from the beginning; so from thence, in all probability, as well as from the evidence of it in universal experience, it was, that the wiser heathen maintained the like doctrine."[81] Here, Edwards shows that certain non-Christian nations are able to discern the things of God because they are universally revealed. Again, it is written on the hearts of the Gentiles.

---

[79] Ibid., 358. Here, Edwards is refuting a specific point made by Taylor.

[80] Ibid., 370.

[81] Ibid., 429n3.

Summary

Edwards believed that all people, regardless of their age, race, status, location, or time in which they were born excluded them from judgment. All stand guilty of sin. They were participants in Adam's sin and they are under the same divine curse. None are innocent and free from the weight of condemnation. God works in human history to vindicate himself as the sovereign Lord over all. He is holy and righteous, judging sin, but he also extends his hand of mercy to the nations. This hope for the nations is seen in Edwards's doctrine of the *prisca theologia*. God has worked in human history to provide a means by which the nations might see exponential revival take over when the gospel is preached. God has worked in the traditions, cultures, and history of the world to bring salvation about when cross-cultural missions occurs. Furthermore, in reading Edwards's treatise, *Original Sin*, he recounts the biblical narrative in such a way that it connects missiology and hamartiology. For example, when he read about the people of Israel conquering non-Christian nations, he saw the purpose as a missional one—to communicate to the nations God's sovereignty and power over other gods. This display of power was meant to persuade the nations to repent and come to Christ for salvation. Also, when Edwards read about the Babylonian exile, the purpose was to communicate to the nations that God is holy and will not allow injustice, unrighteousness, and idolatry to persist, even among his own people. This act of judgment was meant to woe the nations to repent and believe in the gospel. God's working in human history is fundamentally missional.

Thus, Edwards's articulation of the universal depravity of humankind is communicated with a missional vision. Next, we will analyze Edwards's doctrine of the universal ability of humankind. This aspect of his theology of mission will create the possibility of world mission.

Chapter 3
The Universal Ability and Inability of Humankind

This chapter continues our analysis of Edwards's theology of mission by examining his doctrine of the universal ability and inability of humankind. Our first chapter took up Edwards's the foundational component of his theology of world mission, namely, the sovereignty of God. Our second chapter analyzed the need for his theology of world mission, the universal depravity of humankind. The present chapter will look how the previous two chapters remain in tact and yet still allow for the task of world mission. The doctrine of the sovereignty of God maintains the holiness, righteousness, authority, power and transcendence of God. And the doctrine of the universal depravity of humankind maintains that humanity by nature sinful. They are worthy of divine judgment. How is world mission possible with the two are held together? Edwards's doctrine of the universal ability and inability of humankind provides the answer. Our argument in this chapter is that Edwards's doctrine of human ability provides for the possibility of world mission. In other words, Edwards's doctrine the will was often cast within a missional framework.

Our strategy for proving this claim will come in three parts. First, we must establish the intellectual milieu in which Edwards formulated his doctrine of human ability and inability. Edwards sought to answer the Enlightenment questions of the day from a Reformed perspective. This winsome approach allowed him to repackage traditional doctrines in an appealing and persuasive way to his contemporaries. Second, we will identify and explain Edwards's doctrine of universal ability and inability.

This point creatively held together the doctrine of the sovereignty of God and the universal depravity of man and therein created the prospect of world mission. Edwards attempts to resolve this dichotomy by employing this distinction. This distinction vindicates God and condemns humankind while also enabling world mission. Third, we will not only see how Edwards placed this doctrine under the broad rubric of conversion, but also specifically outlined its implications for world mission.

In keeping with our method of presentation, the first section will be a historical-theological analysis of Edwards's doctrine of the universal ability and inability of humankind. The second section will provide a missional reading of Edwards's major treatise—*Freedom of the Will*.

The Possibility for a Theology of Mission: A Historical-Theological Survey

Surveying the Intellectual Milieu

Our first section will provide a survey of the intellectual milieu in which Edwards forged his doctrine of the universal ability and inability of man. This approach will allow us to see the unique contribution Edwards made to the intellectual life of the eighteenth century. To begin, Edwards's doctrine of the universal ability and inability of humankind is self-consciously set against Arminian trends.[1] Edwards saw the Arminian position as a danger to orthodox beliefs. Arminianism was a term used for anyone who assigned any active role to human agency in the process of salvation. They held firm to the conviction that the will be free from any necessity.[2] It must be free to

---

[1] The term Arminianism was imprecise in that it "had become a catch all term for most challenges to strict Calvinist teachings. Although Arminians affirmed that God's grace was essential to salvation, they also believed that people retained some natural ability to choose God's grace or resist it. Salvation was not simply the result of God's sovereign decree from eternity to save some and not others." This general idea is that which Edwards objected to so strenuously. George Marsden, *Jonathan Edwards: A Life*, 86.

[2] The term "necessity" is to be contrasted with another term Edwards frequently used in his discussions of the will–"contingency." "In his treatise *Freedom of the Will* and elsewhere, Edwards used the term 'contingency' when discussing concepts of the will or choice as being dependent on a preexisting cause or condition. In particular, he characterized an Arminian freedom of the will as involving contingency as opposed to necessity. He took contingent acts to be uncaused, unconnected with prior events. Edwards rejected contingency for a variety of reasons." Edwards believed all events to be caused. This idea of contingency was deemed inconsistent with the biblical data surrounding God's foreknowledge and sovereignty. Gregory Rich, "Contingency," in *The Jonathan Edwards Encyclopedia*, eds. Harry S. Stout, Kenneth P. Minkema, and Adriaan C. Neele (Grand Rapids, MI: Eerdmans, 2017).

determine itself. The central issue for Arminians was a concern that if the will is in bondage to sin, human beings can not be held responsible for their sin.

He saw their position as not only wrong, but also contradictory.[3] His answer to this concern was his teaching that distinguished between kinds of ability. His response further developed the Reformed position.[4] This point will be examined in more detail below.

Edwards's articulation of the doctrine of universal inability falls under the larger rubric of conversion. Sinful from birth, God is righteous in his condemnation of human beings. Therefore, they stand in need of forgiveness. As we noted in our previous chapter, Edwards articulated his doctrine from within the Reformed tradition. That tradition claims that humanity is unable to perform any moral good before God. They can do nothing to contribute to their own salvation—-not even the repentance and faith that makes it possible. This Reformed teaching was going out of style in mid-eighteenth century New England. Mark Valeri comments,

> It was commonplace for preachers to say that people were sinners. Edwards appeared to be something of a throwback to the seventeenth century, however, in taking the doctrine to extremes. He asserted not only that people were sinners by nature but also that God judged them guilty and fit for damnation by the depth of depravity that kept them from turning away from sin.[5]

In an age of hopeful optimism for the progress of humanity's achievements, Edwards stood against the tide. Those who questioned the legitimacy of the doctrine objected to its pessimism regarding the natural qualities of man. They believed that "Calvinist doctrine of sin cast an unbecoming shadow

---

[3] Edwards singled out the Arminians' position that the will must be active in determining itself. They said the will simply cannot be passive. He said that if this point is correct, then there is a will that determines the will. "[This argument] is a contradiction; because this supposes an act of the will before the first act determining that. If the will determines its own acts by its own acts, then it determines its own volitions by its volitions. For if the will be determined by an act of the will, 'tis determined by a volition." Edwards, "Miscellanies no. 1155" *WJE* 23:60.

[4] Oliver Crisp highlights that the claim that Edwards developed his doctrine within the Reformed tradition has become a point of debate amongst Edwards scholars. Some believe that Edwards's position was a departure from the Reformed tradition. Oliver Crisp, *Jonathan Edwards Among the Theologians* (Grand Rapids, MI: Eerdmans, 2015), 106.

[5] Mark Valeri, "Editor's Introduction," in *Sermons and Discourses: 1730–1733*, ed. Mark Valeri, vol. 17 of *The Works of Jonathan Edwards* [*WJE*] (New Haven: Yale University Press, 1999), 35.

over God's beneficence and disregarded the natural moral faculties for good that God had implanted in created agents."[6]

The period in which Edwards fashioned his teaching was characterized by a radical shift towards the potential of human achievement. This period, commonly called the Enlightenment, challenged many traditionally held doctrines with this positive view of humanity. Richard A. S. Hall writes of the Enlightenment, "It believed in and acted upon the possibility of human progress, stressed the importance of the here and now as opposed to the hereafter, and had faith in the innate goodness of human beings."[7] This hopeful optimism led many to an Arminian belief that allowed for some role of human agency in conversion.

The Arminian reasoning went as follows: since God was generous, he made every opportunity for human beings to perform morally good actions. Because human beings were born not having performed any righteous or evil deed, they were born neither good nor evil, but with the God-given, innate capacity to do good.[8] Edwards rejected this logic. He argued against any notion that posited an optimistic view of the human condition—especially any notion that might suggest humanity's cooperating in salvation. In one sermon entitled "God Glorified in Man's Dependence," Edwards sought to show man's complete inability to perform any work that might contribute to their salvation. He writes,

> We may here observe the marvelous wisdom of God in the work of redemption. God hath made man's emptiness and misery, his low, lost and ruined state into which he is sunk by the fall, an occasion of the greater advancement of his own glory, as in other ways so particularly in this, that there is now a much more universal and apparent dependence of man on God. Though God be pleased to lift man out of that dismal abyss of sin and woe into which he was fallen, and exceedingly to exalt him in excellency and honor, and to an high pitch of glory and blessedness, yet

---

[6] Ibid.

[7] Richard A. S. Hall, "Enlightenment," in *The Jonathan Edwards Encyclopedia*, eds. Harry S. Stout, Kenneth P. Minkema, and Adriaan C. Neele (Grand Rapids, MI.: Eerdmans, 2017).

[8] Bruce Kuklick writes, "Calvinists believed that humanity was depraved, requiring supernatural grace for salvation. Non-Calvinists parried that individuals were then not responsible, that Calvinists ruled out free will, and that, consequently, God was the author of sin. For the Arminians, the will was not determined. People could be good if they chose; they could respond (or not respond) to grace." Bruce Kuklick, *A History of Philosophy in America 1720–2000* (New York: Oxford University Press, 2001), 20.

the creature has nothing in any respect to glory of; all the glory evidently belongs to God.[9]

Edwards spoke out against "those doctrines and schemes of divinity" which sought to tear down traditional Calvinist orthodoxy.[10] In this text, Edwards assumes humankind can not do anything to contribute to their salvation. Humankind is empty, in misery, and in a ruined state. They are in a "dismal abyss of sin." This emphasis on the universal depravity of humankind is a steadfast affirmation and reinforcement of Reformed anthropology. Humankind is totally corrupt and in need of divine forgiveness.

Any teaching that could emphasize the potential of the creature to the detriment of the sovereignty of God was something to be adamantly rejected. Mark Valeri represents Edwards's belief as follows:

> Those who judge human beings to be not completely depraved grant them independence from God, deny the need for either the Son or the Spirit, and therefore, by implication, reject the Godhead. Any concession to human ability, such as is made by Arminians, amounts to unbelief. Conversely, a doctrine of sin in Calvinist fashion affirms humanity's need for all persons of the Trinity and thereby glorifies God.[11]

Edwards saw the doctrine of human depravity as fundamental to orthodoxy. To accept or reject the traditional teaching was to accept or reject a core tenant of the Christian faith.[12] To Edwards, this teaching is not an issue that is tangential to the gospel, it is part and parcel of it.

---

[9]Edwards delivered this message in a public lecture when many Boston clergymen would have been gathered for the Harvard commencement. This fact is significant because many of those ministers would have been inclined to hold some of the views Edwards denounced. Edwards, "God Glorified in Man's Dependence" *WJE* 17:212.

[10]Ibid.

[11]Mark Valeri, "Editor's Introduction," *WJE* 17:36.

[12]Edwards believed that if one compromised on the doctrine of the will, other fundamental doctrines of the faith were also at risk. Edwards writes, "I stand ready to confess to the forementioned modern divines, if they can maintain their peculiar notion of freedom, consisting in the self-determining power of the will, as necessary to moral agency, and can thoroughly establish it in opposition to the arguments lying against it, then they have an impregnable castle, to which they may repair, and remain invincible, in all the controversies they have with the reformed divines, concerning original sin, the sovereignty of grace, election, redemption, conversion, the efficacious operation of the Holy Spirit, the nature of saving faith, perseverance of the saints, and other principles of the like kind." Edwards, *Original Sin, WJE* 3:376.

Not only does Edwards's sermon uphold the doctrine of universal human depravity, it also upholds the doctrine of the sovereignty of God. Men are dependent on a sovereign God who holds redemption solely within his power. Humankind is totally unable to contribute to salvation. Furthermore, Edwards said that this doctrine pointed towards God's goodness and sovereignty. God alone has the power to redeem. When he does impart salvation, it serves as "an occasion of the greater advancement of his own glory."[13] Man's having to rely on God's goodness and power to save brings glory to God. At the same time, it also uplifts humanity from the "woe into which he has fallen."[14]

Edwards maintained a belief in traditional Calvinist orthodoxy. Yet, Edwards also wanted to present his Reformed belief in a winsome and persuasive way. Instead of staunchly rejecting all elements of Enlightenment optimism, he communicated the doctrine in such a way that applied the hopeful spirit of the movement. Richard A.S. Hall agrees on this point. He writes, "[Edwards] was certainly animated by the spirit of the movement without being chained to its letter. Edwards used philosophical ideas of the Enlightenment in defense and support of Reformed theology and evangelical Calvinism."[15] Edwards sought a solution to the dilemma of human ability that so concerned Enlightenment thinkers. In other words, he sought to answer Enlightenment concerns that the Reformed position took away from humanity's innate freedom and ability.

To be sure, Edwards's answer did not adopt every Enlightenment sentiment or conclusion. For example, some ministers had gone so far as to suggest that good and sincere persons who have never heard the gospel could be saved.[16] Since God was generous and merciful, surely he would graciously judge those who had never heard of Christ. To say otherwise would diminish innate human potential and the moral righteousness of God. But Edwards left no room for this line of reasoning. In an extended Miscellany on the freedom of the will and the issue of "self-determining power," Edwards says, "There is nothing appears in the reason and nature of things ... that can justly lead us to determine that God will certainly

---

[13] Edwards, "God Glorified in Man's Dependence," *WJE* 17:212.

[14] Ibid.

[15] Richard A. S. Hall, "Enlightenment," in *The Jonathan Edwards Encyclopedia*, eds. Harry S. Stout, Kenneth P. Minkema, and Adriaan C. Neele (Grand Rapids, MI.: Eerdmans, 2017).

[16] See Greg D. Gilbert, "The Nations Will Worship: Jonathan Edwards and the Salvation of the Heathen," *TRINJ* 23 (2002): 53–76.

reveal Christ and give the necessary means of grace, or some way or other bestow true holiness and saving grace, and so eternal salvation, to those heathen that are sincere."[17] Not only does Edwards uphold his conception of the universal depravity of humankind, but he also ties it together with his teaching on the moral inability of man. Put simply, Edwards says that regardless of background, race, ethnicity, location vis-à-vis Christendom, individuals are born in sin and completely unable to contribute anything to their salvation because they are willful participants in rebellion against God. Human beings are not born morally or spiritually neutral.

To Edwards, any assertion that distorted the traditional teaching on Original Sin took away a fundamental aspect of the gospel—namely, the very thing that made missions possible. Edwards argued that if mankind was able to contribute to their own salvation, God's advancing his own glory would not be possible.[18] In that case, man would be advancing his own separate kingdom, divergent from that of the kingdom of God. That impossible and alternative reality would be antithetical to the true gospel. To this issue, nothing less than the very glory of God advancing in the world was at stake for Edwards. To say that humankind was capable of contributing anything to salvation was unacceptable. Yet, Edwards creatively answered the spirit of his age with an important distinction that made missions possible.

Natural Ability and Moral Inability

So, what is this distinction that makes world mission possible? Edwards distinguishes between natural and moral ability. This distinction allowed for men to have an innate capacity for fulfilling the divine requirements of the Law, thereby assenting to the Enlightenment's hope for the human condition. But the distinction simultaneously put the emphasis on the traditional Calvinist doctrine, showing that all are willfully disobedient.

Edwards's doctrine can be summarized as follows: a person is completely able to repent, but also unable. In the sense that they are able to repent, this is a natural ability. In the sense that they are unable to repent, this is a spiritual and moral inability. This inability is not due to any natural or

---

[17] Edwards, "Miscellanies no. 1153" *WJE* 23:56.

[18] Edwards writes in one sermon, "Those schemes that put the creature in God's stead ... that exalt man into the place of either Father, Son, or Holy Ghost, in anything pertaining to our redemption ... and whatever other way any scheme is inconsistent with our entire dependence on God for all, and in each of those ways, of having all of him, through him, and in him, it is repugnant to the design and tenor of the gospel, and robs it of that which God accounts its luster and glory." Edwards, *Sermons and Discourses, 1730–1733*, *WJE* 17:212–3.

physical limitations placed on the person. If a person was constrained by any outside force, that person would not be held liable to judgment. This inability springs forth from an inner, moral obstruction. Individuals are born with an innate moral obstinacy. They do not want to please God. They are born with a hard heart, unwilling to keep the commands of God. Humans naturally want to disbelieve and disobey God.

Therefore, Edwards believes humanity has free will because they are able to choose what they want. Edwards defines his terms carefully to achieve such a conclusion. He writes, "Thus an act of the will is commonly expressed by its pleasing a man to do thus or thus; and a man's doing as he wills, and doing as he pleases, are the same thing in common speech."[19] Whatever a person pleases to do, he or she is able to do. There are no outside forces preventing a person from making whatever choice which they desire to make. Edwards continues, "A man never, in any instance, wills anything contrary to his desires, or desires anything contrary to his will."[20] For Edwards, the will and the person are inseparable. He writes, "In every act, or going forth of the will, there is some preponderance of the mind or inclination, one way rather than another; and the soul had rather have or do one thing than another."[21] In a person's choosing of a thing, they always choose the "greatest apparent good."[22]

Again, Edwards rejects the Arminian notion that a person is in a "state of perfect indifference."[23] Allen Guelzo elaborates Edwards's point here,

> To will is not to choose in a vacuum, or ... to choose choosing. To will is to perform an act of volition, caused by motives which move the understanding and will together to an intelligent choice ... The will is not free to choose what to will; freedom consists only in willing as a man is "pleased." To conceive of freedom of the will as an internal, uncaused, autonomous function can only land the Arminian in the position of excluding any good or bad motives from choice lest the will's freedom be endangered; or, if good or bad motives do happen to creep in, to withhold

---

[19] Jonathan Edwards, *Freedom of the Will*, ed. Paul Ramsey, vol. 1 of *The Works of Jonathan Edwards* [*WJE*] (New Haven: Yale University Press, 1970), 139.

[20] Ibid.

[21] Edwards, *Freedom of the Will*, WJE 1:140.

[22] Ibid., 142.

[23] Ibid., 140.

praise from any resulting good acts, and excuse any resulting bad ones.[24]

Edwards firmly asserts that a person is bound by their own desires. Moreover, this connection between individuals and their desires is what makes them susceptible to praise or judgment. In other words, Edwards believes this understanding of the will allows a person to be held accountable for their own choices.

Edwards's doctrine of natural ability means that a person is free to choose whatever it is they want according to their physical or natural capacity. On the contrary, Edwards's doctrine of moral inability means that the natural man (that is, the unconverted person) is not free to choose what is really good. Edwards makes this point in a comment on Romans 7:4.[25] He writes, "Hence we may argue that there is no lawful child brought forth before that marriage. Seeming virtues and good works before, are not so indeed; they are a spurious brood, being bastards and not children."[26] Humans, in their natural condition, are unable to do anything pleasing to God. Their "virtues and good works" before conversion are worthless in God's sight. These unrighteous actions flow out of their sinful nature. This state is one they have been with from birth. Edwards draws sharp and clear lines on how God would view such an action. He writes, "Everything that we do that is not part of God's service is part of the devil's service."[27] Either an action is good and pleasing to God, or it is odious to him. The overwhelming thrust of Edwards's teaching on humankind's natural ability is that of inability. Every person born of Adam is incapable of pleasing God.[28] This point flows out of our previous chapter's discussion of the doctrine of *Original Sin*. The opening line of that treatise affirms Edwards's belief in an "innate sinful depravity of the human heart."[29]

---

[24] Allen Guelzo, *Edwards on the Will: A Century of American Theological Debate* (Middletown, CT: Wesleyan University Press, 1989), 53. Italics original.

[25] Romans 7:4 reads, "Wherefore, my brethren, ye also are become dead to the law by the body of Christ; that ye should be married to another, even to him who is raised from the dead, that we should bring forth fruit unto God."

[26] Jonathan Edwards, *The "Miscellanies": (Entry Nos. 501–832)*, WJE 18:498.

[27] Jonathan Edwards, *Sermons and Discourses: 1720–1723*, ed. Wilson H. Kimnach, vol. 10 of *The Works of Jonathan Edwards* [WJE] (New Haven: Yale University Press, 1992), 487.

[28] Edwards did speculate that it is probable that "few infants are converted in infancy." His "Miscellanies" no. 816 expounds on the possibility of salvation in infancy. Ibid., 526.

[29] Edwards, *Original Sin*, WJE 3:107.

In most places throughout his writings, Jonathan Edwards ties this topic of human ability and volition together with the extensive topic of conversion. However, there are select places where one sees this couched in explicitly missional language.[30] Again, our definition of mission is broadly about the advancement of the kingdom of God on earth. Yet, special attention is given to the advancement of the Christian religion into areas beyond Christendom. Therefore, the research presented here will focus broadly on the doctrine of conversion—which the topic of world mission falls underneath that broader rubric—but particular consideration will be given to language that includes missional terms and concepts.

Edwards draws this distinction most clearly and extensively in his treatise *Freedom of the Will*. However, his *Treatise on Grace* reveals the origin and background for his thoughts on this distinction. In this work, Edwards places this discussion under the larger rubric of divine grace. Edwards attempts to prove from an analysis of particular biblical verses that it is God alone who gives grace. Humans do not conjure up within themselves a desire to do good. All moral good comes from God. Edwards starts his presentation of texts from the beginning of the Bible and then lists them in order until the end. In most cases, Edwards simply lists the text without comment or qualification. The text is meant to stand alone in support his argument. Yet, some of the texts have comment. These explanations give insight as to Edwards's main point regarding human willpower. For example, remarks on Proverbs 21:1.[31] Edwards writes,

> Here it is represented as though the will of God determined the wills of men, and that when God was pleased to interpose, he ever directs them according to his pleasure without fail in any instance. This shows that God has not left men's hearts so in their own hands as to be determined by themselves alone, independent on any antecedent determination.[32]

---

[30] Missional language is meant to include explicit and implicit concepts that speak about the advancement of the Christian religion, especially into areas outside Christendom. One typically encounters missional language when Edwards speaks of the "heathen," "pagan," "Gentile nations," and other such terms that talk about people outside of Israel or the church.

[31] "The king's heart is in the hand of the Lord, as the rivers of water: he turneth it whithersoever he will." Proverbs 21:1

[32] Jonathan Edwards, *Writings on the Trinity, Grace, and Faith*, ed. Sang Huyn Lee, vol. 21 of *The Works of Jonathan Edwards* [WJE] (New Haven: Yale University Press, 2003), 254.

God is one who ultimately governs the actions of men. It is not as though humans are uninhibited in their choices. In other words, they do not possess a will that is totally unrestricted of any predisposition. In fact, God is the one who shapes and guides their moral choices. To be sure, Edwards follows in the Reformed tradition in his affirmation that mystery exists in this scheme. He also follows the tradition's denial that God is the author of evil.[33] There is no injustice in God. In his "Miscellany," no. 763, Edwards writes clearly, "[God] really desires the conversion and salvation of reprobates, and laments their obstinacy and misery."[34] Thus, Edwards places the blame totally on the sinner for their wrongdoing. What Edwards means to say is that all morally acceptable, good, and righteous actions are considered a gift from God. The source and substance of all goodness found in man is of God. When humans choose evil, they do so because they want to do so. These choices spring from their own fallen condition. Again, Edwards's emphasis here is that all good choices are a gift from God. No one is able to take credit for their turning towards God.

In the next verse listed–Proverbs 28:26–he says, "A man is to be commended for making a wise improvement of his outward possessions, for his own comfort, but yet 'tis the gift of God."[35] It may appear that a person makes a good choice out of his own self, but it is entirely a gift from God. The one who ultimately receives credit for the righteous act is God.

Summarizing Edwards's doctrine, David Bebbington writes,

> On the Edwardsean view, sinners possessed a natural ability to believe the gospel, so that nothing in the capacities with which they had been endowed by their Creator prevented them from becoming Christians. What they might display, however, was a moral inability to embrace the gospel, an expression of refusal to repent of their sins, which was their own fault. Consequently, all human beings had an obligation to accept salvation, and every minister could proclaim the gospel without reservation. Ed-

---

[33] Edwards explicit rejects the claim that God is the author of evil in the conclusion to his treatise. Edwards, *Freedom of the Will*, WJE 1:434–5.

[34] Edwards, "Miscellanies no. 763" *WJE* 18:410.

[35] Ibid.; "He that trusteth in his own heart is a fool: but whoso walketh wisely, he shall be delivered." Proverbs 28:26

wards's central theological teaching provided hitherto inhibited Calvinists with a new and pressing sense of mission.[36]

Bebbington relates the point to world mission by saying humans have a natural capacity to repent and believe. Thus, the church can preach in such a way that unbelievers may immediately experience conversion. While Edwards often spoke generally about ability and inability under the broad rubric of conversion, he did make direct connections to world mission.

Missional Connection

Again, Edwards puts this doctrine of divine sovereignty and human inability in missional terms. One sees this evangelistic impetus throughout his writings. One of the clearest places we see this is in his *Treatise on Grace*, Book III. In this section of the treatise, Edwards is pointing to specific Scripture passages that highlight the doctrine of efficacious grace in opposition to the Arminian teaching on the will. He begins by saying that God has promised "that great revival of religion in the latter days."[37] But this promise can only be good if God is sovereign over all things, including the choices of men. The Arminian position can not guarantee the outcome of promise.[38] Only the Reformed position can guarantee a sure outcome because it sees God as dispensing grace that achieves its desired outcome. But what is the promise? Edwards says it is no less than the salvation of the nations.

> God promises Abraham that all the families of the earth shall be blessed in him. God swears that every knee should bow and every tongue confess. And it is said to [be] given to Christ that every nation and language should serve and obey him (Dan. 7:14). After what manner they shall serve and obey him is abundantly declared in other prophecies, as Is. 11 and innumerable others. They are spoken of in the next chapter, ch. 12, as the "excellent things" that God does.

---

[36] D.W. Bebbington, "The Reputation of Edwards Abroad," In *The Cambridge Companion to Jonathan Edwards,* ed. Stephen J. Stein (New York: Cambridge University Press, 2007), 246.

[37] Edwards, *Writings on the Trinity, Grace, and Faith, WJE* 21:256.

[38] Edwards writes, "And how can [God] promise, as he oftentimes does in his Word, glorious times when righteousness shall generally prevail and his will shall generally be done, and yet it is not an effect that it belongs to him to determine? 'Tis not left to his determination, but to the sovereign arbitrary determination of others, independent on any determination of him. And therefore surely they ought [not] to be promises. For him to promise that has it not in his hands to dispose and determine is a great absurdity." Ibid., 242–3.

God's promise for the success of world mission depends on his ability to sovereignly and effectually work salvation. If salvation depended on a free will that was independent and autonomous from the person's nature, none should be converted.[39] Edwards goes on draw connections to mission, "How often is the faith of the Gentiles, or their coming into the Christian church, promised to Christ in the Old Testament (Is. 49:6 and many other places); and he has promised it to his church (ch. 49:18–21 and innumerable other places). See Rom. 15:12–13."[40] God has promised that the nations will experience salvation, and he will see to it that it is accomplished.

After making this connection, Edwards lists numerous instances of Scriptures that draw out this link between efficacious grace and world mission. For example, Edwards points to the Synoptic Gospels' account of Jesus telling his disciples they will be fishers of men. He says that the fishing for men "was wholly his doings and was ascribed to him."[41] The meaning here is that the disciples will evangelize the people, but ultimately, God will be the one who is working. Here, Edwards places the source of salvation in God alone. In other words, the nations will only find salvation in God. Another passage Edwards references in support is Luke 3:8, which reads, "God is able of these stones to raise up children unto Abraham." Here, the emphasis is God's sovereignty in bringing about salvation to the Gentile nations.

In what is quite possibly the clearest connection of missions and human ability is his listing of John 12:31–32 with Psalm 2:8.[42] Edwards lists these passages as support for his claim that God's promise to redeem the nations depends on his sovereignty over all things. In the numerous passages previously listed, the main point was to highlight God's sovereignty and man's total dependency on God for salvation. Now, Edwards begins to more clearly connect these two themes to world mission. He moves from the broad theme of conversion to the narrower subject of world mission. God will effectually draw the nations unto himself so that they might experience

---

[39] Edwards refutes Henry Stebbing at multiple points in this treatise. Stebbing wrote a book on the Holy Spirit that Edwards interacted with as representative of the Arminian position. "Stebbing owns that, on their principles, conversion depending on the determination of free will, it is possible in its own nature that none should ever be converted." Ibid., 243.

[40] Ibid.

[41] Ibid., 256.

[42] John 12:31–21 reads, "Now is the judgment of this world: now shall the prince of this world be cast out. And I, if I be lifted up from the earth, will draw all men unto me." Psalm 2:8 reads, "Ask of me, and I shall give thee the heathen for thine inheritance, and the uttermost parts of the earth for thy possession." Ibid., 257.

salvation. The subjects of this divine grace will be the non-Christian nations. The non-Christian nations will be given to the Messiah as an inheritance.

Edwards goes on to cite Acts 15:3–4 in support, "Declaring the conversion of the Gentiles ... and they declared all things that God had done with them." The salvation of the unbeliever and the verbal proclamation of God's sovereignty is celebrated in these verses. He immediately then refers to Romans 9 and connects mission with this dichotomy between divine and human abilities, "'Tis God that preserves the remnant, and that it [is] of the election of his grace or free kind[ness], and not of their works, but in such a way of freedom as is utterly inconsistent with its being of their works; and in v. 7, that it is not determined by their seeking but God's election."[43] Men are saved not by their works or their seeking, but only by the free grace of God. They simply cannot freely choose to follow God and decide purse righteousness on their own. It must be granted to them by God. One cannot simply conjure up within themselves the desire to do the good and follow through on that feeling. Here, we see Edwards connecting missions under the broader rubric of conversion.

Furthermore, Edwards references 1 Corinthians 3:5–9 where Paul speaks of the dynamic of Christian ministry in agrarian terms. He compares what Scripture says against the Arminian teaching.

> According to the Arminian scheme it ought to have been, "I have planted, and Apollos watered, and God hath planted and watered more especially: for we have done it only as his servants. But you yourselves have given the increase; the fruit has been left to your free will," according to what the Arminians from time to time insist, in what they say upon the parable of the vineyard which God planted in a fruitful hill, etc. and "looked that it should bring forth grapes," and says, "What could I have done more to my vineyard?"[44]

According to the Arminian teaching, one has the natural and moral ability to freely choose good. Therefore, humans freely cooperate with God in ministry. God receives the primary place in this system, but men are also included in the accomplishing of the task. Edwards shows the folly of this scheme by intentional twisting the Scripture to say something it obviously does not. Humans can not take the credit for the fruit of good works because

[43] Ibid., 257.
[44] Ibid., 259.

it is ultimately God who is the one who gives them the will and power to do it.

For Edwards, world mission is made possible because of God's power to work in the lives of human beings. He held to the Reformed emphasis on the sovereignty of God in salvation. Moreover, human beings are unable to appropriately respond to the gospel message. Left alone, human beings cannot conjure up within themselves repentance and faith in Christ. This fact is due to their sinful nature. Also, Edwards expressed this doctrine in universal terms. This teaching is his doctrine of the universal inability of humankind. Yet, Edwards simultaneously captured the Enlightenment ethos of human potentiality. He taught that human beings are in some sense capable of responding positively to the gospel message. There are no physical or external barriers preventing them from appropriately responding. The nations may immediately experience salvation when they hear the gospel preached because they possess a natural ability to respond. Therefore, the possibility of missions exists because "God is willing to save to sinners."[45] He is sovereign, even over hard hearts. Edwards writes, "We are dependent on God's power through every step of our redemption. We are dependent on the power of God to convert us, and give faith in Jesus Christ, and the new nature."[46] When the gospel message goes out to the nations, they are capable of responding to it. Yet, God is the one who is sovereign over their salvation. For Edwards, teaching on the will makes world mission possible.

Freedom of the Will: A Missional Reading

Following up from our last chapter's treatment of Edwards's treatise *Original Sin,* we now turn our attention to another major treatise Edwards wrote during his cross-cultural missionary experience in Stockbridge—*Freedom of the Will.*[47] Finished in 1754, Edwards finally completed this massive project.

---

[45] Edwards, "Death and Judgment" in *Sermons and Discourses, 1743–1758, WJE* 25:597.

[46] Jonathan Edwards, "God Glorified in Man's Dependence" in *Sermons and Discourses, 1730–1733, WJE* 17: 205.

[47] While not directly related to our thesis, one need not miss the relevance of his historical context. Edwards articulated his ideas in the midst of a missional environment. During that season of ministry, Edwards was preaching to the Mohican and Housatonic Indians on a regular basis. At great personal cost to himself, he was advocating for the Indian school in Stockbridge. For a detailed account of this struggle, see Marsden, *Jonathan Edwards: A Life.* In short, Edwards spoke out against the exploitation and abuses against the Native American population by some of the British colonists. Much of his conflict would have been against those associated with William Williams and his family.

Edwards began the work much earlier, but the completion of the work was delayed due to the untimely death of David Brainerd. He picked up the work in 1747, but was delayed again due to a controversy in his church.[48] This attentiveness to return to this project shows how Edwards saw the importance of the subject. He thought deeply about this topic throughout the course of his life.

Edwards believed the issue of the freedom of the will was at the heart of biblical Christianity. He felt compelled to speak against the contemporary notions of the day. McClymond and McDermott write, "Jonathan Edwards thought a misunderstanding of the human will was at the root of nearly all that had gone wrong in theology."[49] Similarly, Ramsey writes, "For Edwards the refutation of Arminian notions of free will was the thing upon which hinged everything else of importance for the religious thought of his century, as the impression of grace upon the soul was the foundation of the religious life."[50] Placing great importance on this specific doctrine, Edwards sought to dismantle Arminian notions of free will and articulate a creative response that fell within the boundaries of traditional Reformed teaching.[51] The Arminian system held that human beings are totally free in their choices. Their choices are not determined by any outside forces. The will is indifferent to any particular choice prior to the decision made.[52] Moreover, a person

---

[48] This controversy was the communion controversy, which would eventually lead to his dismissal from the Northampton pulpit. Marsden, *Jonathan Edwards: A Life*, 436–7.

[49] Gerald McClymond and Michael McClymond, *The Theology of Jonathan Edwards* (New York: Oxford University Press, 2012), 339.

[50] Edwards, *Freedom of the Will, WJE* 1:70.

[51] Joe Rigney says, "In Edwards's mind, there was an integral connection between one's view of the will and one's view of a host of important theological doctrines: God's foreknowledge and providence, human sin and corruption, saving grace and election. If the Arminian doctrine of the will was overthrown and the Calvinist doctrine established, then Edwards believed that the entire Arminian project—ubiquitous in England and increasing in the colonies—would crumble." Edwards's refutation of the Arminian doctrine would take away the foundation for many other doctrines that were deviations from the Reformed system. Therefore, Edwards's treatment of this subject would also have implications for other key areas of theology. For our purposes, we will analyze the relevant conclusions for conversion and its cross-cultural corollary–world mission. Joe Rigney, In "Freedom of the Will," *A Reader's Guide to the Major Writings of Jonathan Edwards,* eds. Nathan A. Finn and Jeremy Kimble (Wheaton, IL; Crossway, 2017), 133.

[52] Scott Oliphant writes, "One of Edwards' most insistent principles is the absurdity of supposing the will to be indifferent. Edwards will not tolerate such assumed neutrality. In his battle with the Arminians one of the primary tenets of their approach to 'free will' was the will's indifference, a tenet which Edwards annihilates in his book Freedom of the Will." Scott Oliphant, "Jonathan Edwards: Reformed Apologist," *The Westminster Theological Journal* 57 (1995): 171.

has a fully self-determining power to accept or reject all potential choices.[53] This scheme, the Arminian teaching maintained, was the only possible scenario in which men were able to be held fully responsible for their choices. Conversely, Edwards maintained that his doctrine allowed for men to be held fully responsible for their actions, while also maintaining the Reformed teaching of God's sovereignty over all things. Edwards's position in the treatise is accurately and succinctly put by Oliver Crisp. He writes, "Edwards's main concern in the treatise *Freedom of the Will* was to show that only a version of compatibilism (the doctrine according to which human free will is compatible with determinism, in this case divine determinism) was theologically viable."[54] For Edwards, this approach allowed for and gave implications for world mission. Again, our purpose in providing a missional reading of this treatise is not to provide a summary of the treatise or trace the detailed contours of Edwards's logic, but to highlight the themes that directly intersect with world mission. We will follow this missional reading with some additional context surrounding the treatise which will add to our understanding of what Edwards is trying to do from a mission standpoint.

The Possibility for Mission

The primary purpose of Edwards's treatise is to identify and repudiate the foundation of the Arminian position. He wants to expose its error, present a constructive account of how the will actually functions, and work through some of its implications. He does this because he sees the Arminian teaching at a threat to genuine conversion—-and, therefore, world mission. He begins by identifying the heart of his contention with the Arminian position. He asks the following question: How are human beings to be held morally responsible by God for their actions? Crisp and Strobel write of Edwards's treatise,

---

[53] Garrett Pendergraft succinctly characterizes Edwards's summary of the Arminian teaching on free will. Edwards believed that the Arminian taught that "doing what one wills was necessary for freedom, but not sufficient." Furthermore, there are three essential conditions on freedom "1. The will must determine itself. 2. The will must not be determined by anything outside itself. 3. Choices must be made in a state of indifference." It is these three conditions and the implications that they produce which Edwards seeks to challenge and refute. Garrett Pendergraft, "Freedom of the Will (Doctrine)," in *The Jonathan Edwards Encyclopedia*, eds. Harry S. Stout, Kenneth P. Minkema, and Adriaan C. Neele (Grand Rapids, MI.: Eerdmans, 2017). Italics Original. These three points are derived and reworded from Edwards's three points listed in Part One. There are listed here instead of Edwards's original words because they are more clearly and succinctly written. They accurately reflect Edwards's meaning. Edwards, *Freedom of the Will,* 1:164–5.

[54] Oliver Crisp, *Jonathan Edwards Among the Theologians* (Grand Rapids: Eerdmans, 2015), 87.

His treatise *Freedom of the Will* is a massive attempt to refute the claim that one must be free in the sense required by synchronistic contingency if one is to be morally responsible for one's actions ... The main point of contention is moral responsibility. The issue of what sort of freedom of will is required in order for a person to be held morally accountability for her or his action."[55]

The Arminian position claims that one must have a will that has the freedom to equally choose one thing or the other. In other words, equal weight must be given to all potential choices and there cannot be any predisposition (or condition) of the person that might incline them towards one choice over and against another. Oliver Crisp summarizes Edwards's complaint against the Arminian view.

> Edwards is clear that libertarian free will is no free will at all ... As far as Edwards is concerned, an uncaused choice is not a free choice at all but a random, inexplicable event. Clearly such events are not ones for which a person can be morally responsible. So libertarianism actually eviscerates moral responsibility by removing causation from the notion of a truly free choice. By contrast, compatibilism makes sense of moral responsibility because it conjoins cause and desire ... Where action is caused by the strongest motive and desire, a person acts freely.[56]

Edwards's point is to show how the will and person are interconnected. Crisp writes of Edwards's position, "There is no faculty of the will somehow *distinct* from the agent that wills ... the agent is the one who wills, and the will is just a way of speaking about certain sorts of actions the agent performs."[57] Instead of asking if the will is free, one must ask if the person is free. If the person is bound by their own sin since before their birth, then necessarily, the will is not free to choose in the libertarian sense of how freedom is defined. According to Edwards, individuals are controlled by their own sinful desires. Furthermore, they are morally responsible for their sinful actions because there is an antecedent cause to their choice—-namely,

---

[55] Oliver Crisp and Kyle Strobel, *Jonathan Edwards: An Introduction to His Thought* (Grand Rapids, MI: Eerdmans, 2018), 117.

[56] Ibid., 104.

[57] Ibid., 88.

their own carnal inclination to choose that evil thing. In short, humankind is sinful and in bondage to that sin.

One aspect of Edwards's central claim is that God is both omnipotent over all things and omniscient of all things—-including human agency. In speaking of the will, Edwards writes, "For, as the being of the world is from God, so the circumstances in which it had its being at first, both negative and positive, must be ordered by him ... and all the necessary consequences of these circumstances, must be ordered by him."[58] To be consistent with these qualities, one must see all events as caused by a moral agent. In the case of human beings, their choices are determined by their own will. These choices are entirely consistent with God's sovereignty. As Edwards works to prove this claim, he explicitly seeks to refute the Arminian position by showing its absurdity in connection to the traditional attributes of God. Again, Edwards views God's sovereignty from a Reformed perspective. Furthermore, Edwards connects a Reformed understanding of God's foreknowledge to the theme of world mission. In an extensive section outlining this connection, Edwards says that this connection is seen throughout all of Scripture. "Hence that great promise and oath of God to Abraham, Isaac and Jacob... that in their seed all the nations and families of the earth should be blessed, must be made on uncertainties, if God don't certainly foreknow the volitions of moral agents."[59] In other words, God's promises are as good as his knowledge of future events. If God does not know the future—-namely, the choices of human beings—with absolute certainty, the promises he made to the patriarchs are subject to doubt. They are questionable and one cannot fully rely on them. Maybe they will be fulfilled. Maybe they will not. According to Edwards, God's promise of "setting up of his spiritual kingdom over the nations of the world" is based on his foreknowledge of future events.[60] Therefore, the promises of God can be trusted. Edwards goes on to quote specific verses that assure God's victory over the idolatry and unchristian practices of Gentile nations.[61] He also goes into very specific detail to include the choices of non-Christian kings and nations.[62]

---

[58] Edwards, *Freedom of the Will*, WJE 1:432.

[59] Ibid., 247.

[60] Ibid.

[61] Specifically, he quotes Psalm 72:11, 17 and Micah 7:19, 20. These verses envision a future day when all kings and nations will bow down to Christ in worship. All nations of the earth will rise up to serve him.

[62] Edward seeks to show the dizzying absurdity of God's predictions if he did not really know the results of future choices and events. There is no way that anyone—no matter how

Furthermore, Edwards champions the Reformed position because he believes it upholds the supreme sovereignty of God in a way that the Arminian view simply cannot. He writes,

> According to the scheme I am endeavoring to confute, neither the fall of men nor angels, could be foreseen, and God must be greatly disappointed in these events; and so the grand scheme and contrivance for our redemption, and destroying the works of the devil ... must be only the fruits of his own disappointment, and contrivances of his to mend and patch up ... but was marred, broken and confounded by the free will of angels and men. And still he must be liable to be totally disappointed a second time: he could not know, that he should have his desired success, in the incarnation, life, death, resurrection and exaltation of his only begotten Son ... he could not know after all, whether there would actually be any tolerable measure of restoration; for this depended on the free will of man."[63]

Here, Edwards shows that in the Arminian scheme, God is a being to be pitied. He had noble and good intentions in his original creation. He has worked greatly in the world, but he is frustrated by the world he created—both the choices of men and angels. Moreover, he is frustrated by the fact that he cannot know whether or not his attempts to fix the problem will actually work. He must hope for the best. He does not have full governing control over either men or angels. Therefore, God's happiness is subject to the choices of his created beings. Since God could not foresee the choices man and angels would have made, he is saddened by their free choices. In short, God is unsatisfied because limited in his foreknowledge and power.

Immediately after making this point, Edwards makes the connection between God's sovereignty and foreknowledge to world mission.

> There has been a general great apostasy of almost all the Christian world, to that which was worse than heathenism; which

---

powerful—could accurately predict the millions upon millions of choices by people and due to the seemingly infinite number of possible outcomes based on even just one choice. While Edwards lists godly kings of Israel and Judah, he also lists Gentile kings and rulers such as Nebuchadnezzar, Cyrus, Alexander, Pompey, and Julius Caesar. Edwards, *Freedom of the Will*, 249.

[63] Ibid., 255–6.

continued for many ages. And how could God, without foreseeing men's volitions, know whether ever Christendom would return from this apostasy? ...how could it be known that the gospel, which was not effectual for the reformation of the Jews, would ever be effectual for the turning of the heathen nations from their heathen apostasy, which they had been confirmed in for so many ages?[64]

Edwards is saying that God really does know the future. Just as he can prophesy that Christendom would experience a great reversal in their condition, he can also predict that the non-Christian nations will repent and turn to Christ for salvation. He is sovereign over all things, including the free choices of all humankind. The gospel of Jesus Christ will be effective in its proclamation in the non-Christian nations because God stands over time and he knows the beginning from the end. He says that God made the world for himself, created it for his own good pleasure, and caused it to "infallibly obtain his end."[65] Edwards holds that the Arminian logic is completely inconsistent with the biblical data. Any notion that seeks to frustrate God or his plans is to be rejected. Conversely, Edwards's scheme places God's sovereignty at the center—-even of human free will.

God's sovereignty is maintained and human responsibility being upheld can be most clearly seen in Edwards's most famous analogy. This analogy is especially important when viewed from a missional perspective.[66] In the analogy, there are multiple images and variations, but a singular point. Edwards says that God is not like one who calls for a person who has lost his legs to walk. It would be unreasonable to condemn that person for failing to live up to the command because they are naturally unable to perform that task. Similarly, God is not like one who calls for a prisoner, bound in unbreakable chains within strong walls and behind a heavy gate, to come forth and escape. This line of reasoning is the Arminian critique against the Reformed view on free will. However, Edwards refutes this line of thinking by distinguishing between two different types of ability—natural and moral. In the Arminian critique of the Reformed view, God would be unjust to condemn someone who has no ability to respond freely and appropriately. But that is not a true picture of what is actually happening. The lame person

---

[64] Ibid., 256.

[65] Ibid.

[66] Ibid., 362–3.

is physically unable to perform the task. The prisoner is naturally incapable to break free. He might be willing to escape. He might be repentant of his wrongdoing, but he cannot escape because of the external, impenetrable barriers preventing him from doing so.

Instead, the proper way of viewing this scenario, according to Edwards, is of a compassionate king and an indignant prisoner. The compassionate king order that the doors be flung open and his chains cast off. If he wishes to be released, he must come out and ask for forgiveness. But the prisoner is obstinate. He will not apologize to the king and ask for forgiveness. He is so prideful that he cannot humble himself and bring himself to repentance. Therefore, in some sense, he is unable to escape. For Edwards, to say that a person is unable to achieve salvation must be nuanced so that important distinctions can be readily seen. The person is completely able to exit the prison because there is no exterior or natural barrier preventing him. It is only due to the prisoner's recalcitrant pride that prevents him from freedom. Edwards calls his inner agency a moral ability.[67]

As it relates to the concept of salvation (and therefore conversion and world mission) a person—regardless of their background, race, ethnicity, etc.,—is able to come to saving faith in Christ in that there are no natural obstacles or impediments that prevents them from it. The non-Christian nations are unable to repent and come to Christ in the sense that all humankind has an inner obstinacy of the heart. They are unwilling to repent and turn to Christ for salvation. They are unable to bring themselves to repentance and faith because of their hardheartedness. To be saved, God must be the one who acts in their heart. God is the one who gives them a heart to repent. In short, Edwards's distinction of natural and moral ability shows the impossibility of world missions—if the person is left alone to their own choices. Yet, on the contrary, if a person is left to God's good will and pleasure, that place is the only possibility for world mission.[68]

---

[67] To give a modern example to highlight the point, if a rebellious (and able-bodied) teenager is asked by their parent to clean their room, they would be considered physically able to perform the task, but unwilling. Thus, it may be said that they are physically able to perform the task. There is nothing restricting their physical ability to perform the task. Yet, they are unwilling to obey because of their rebellious nature.

[68] Edwards views salvation as wholly from God's grace. He writes, "The conversion of a sinner being not owing to a man's self-determination, but to God's determination, and eternal election, which is absolute, and depending on the sovereign will of God, and not on the free will of man." Edwards, *Freedom of the Will*, 1:436.

Missional Concerns Behind the Text

In the year that Edwards wrote this treatise, he wrote a letter to his transatlantic correspondent John Erskine. In that letter, he explicitly connected the entire distinction of moral ability and natural ability to the doctrine of conversion. This connection helps us see the missional concern behind the treatise itself. He begins his argument by connecting a person's ability to God's sovereignty. He says that a person praying for another's conversion is useless if God is not sovereign over all of salvation. Why would someone pray to God? In the Arminian scheme, God has done all that he can and will ever do. To infringe on a person's will would be unacceptable in the Arminian system because to do so would invade in upon the independence of their creaturely agency.

> This notion of self-dependence and self-determination, tends to prevent or enervate all prayer to God for converting grace; for why should men earnestly cry to God for his grace, to determine their hearts to that, which they must be determined to of themselves? And indeed it destroys the very notion of conversion itself. There can properly be no such thing, or anything akin to what the Scripture speaks of as conversion, renovation of the heart, regeneration, etc. if growing good by a number of successive self-determined acts, be all that is required, or to be expected.[69]

Again, we see Edwards's thought process underlying the concepts articulated in his *Freedom of the Will*. His concern is related to the lived experience of the common believer. From reading the letter, one sees a passionate theologian who is concerned about the people to whom he is ministering. He says that he writes these issues "from the fullness of [his] heart." He has "long seen of the dreadful consequences of these prevalent notions everywhere." And it "fills [him] with great concern."[70] He has seen and experienced the effects of misinterpreting this doctrine and these errors have grieved him.

Edwards's letter to John Erskine succinctly summarizes the missional heart behind his academic treatise. Whereas *Freedom of the Will* focuses

---

[69] Jonathan Edwards, *Letters and Personal Writings,* ed. George S. Claghorn, vol. 16 of *The Works of Jonathan Edwards* [WJE] (New Haven: Yale University Press, 1998), 722.

[70] Ibid., 723.

largely on the highly complex philosophy and logic behind the issue, the letter written to Erskine reflects Edwards's practical concerns in terms of how they play out in evangelism and missions. In that letter, he says that the only way a person can be held morally responsible for their actions is according to his compatibilist scheme. He writes, "I think the notion of liberty, consisting in a contingent self-determination of the will, as necessary to the morality of men's dispositions and actions."[71] Edwards reflects on his many years of ministry and reveals his missional concern—-the salvation of sinners.

> The longer I live, and the more I have to do with the souls of men in the work of the ministry, the more I see of this. Notions of this sort are one of the main hindrances of the success of the preaching of the Word, and other means of grace, in the conversion of sinners. This especially appears when the minds of sinners are affected with some concern for their souls, and they are stirred up to seek their salvation.[72]

One of the main obstacles Edwards sees against true conversion is a person's insistence that they do what they can. They try their best, but still can not help improve their condition. There is nothing that they can do but simply try their best. Edwards concludes, "Things of this kind have visibly been the main hindrance of the true humiliation and conversion of sinners, in the times of awakening, that have been in this land, everywhere, in all parts, as I have had opportunity to observe in very many places."[73] Edwards places his concerns within the context, not just of ministry in polite European society, but also "everywhere," "in all parts," and in "very many places." Whereas one might conclude the reference is primarily referring to areas that have been settled by colonialists (and therefore white Europeans), one must consider the possibility that Edwards has an eye toward the Native Americans. This conclusion is not simply a possibility, but it is a probability when one considers the historical context in which this letter (and treatise) is written. Edwards is daily ministering amongst the Housatonic and Mohawk population of Western Massachusetts. Apparently he sees how false ideas surrounding the idea of free will have adversely effected the impact on evangelism and world mission.

[71] Ibid., 719.
[72] Ibid.
[73] Ibid., 721.

In summary, Edwards perceives that other notions of free will and grace prevent sinners from earnestly seeking their own salvation. Edwards's letter from beginning to end expresses concern that men are not interested in salvation because they lack the ability to do anything that might improve their condition. Therefore, Edwards's rigorous philosophical conclusions regarding natural and moral ability have great pastoral concerns as they relate to the salvation of everyday people.

Summary

In the generation after his death, Edwards's successors would capitalize on his teaching.[74] They would highlight its usefulness in revival by stressing the immediacy of repentance. One of the most distinct features of the so-called New Divinity Movement is its furthering of Edwards's teaching on universal ability and inability in preaching the gospel. Robert Caldwell writes, "The *voluntarist accent* in Edwards's thought, most notably his understanding of natural ability, translated into the New Divinity's emphasis on *immediate repentance*."[75] One would instantaneously repent of their sins and trust in Christ for salvation. There was no need for a protracted conversion process in which one needed to go through certain steps in order to be saved. One could immediately see their sinful condition and repent because there are no external or natural barriers preventing them from coming to faith in Christ. In effect, Edwards's immediate successors saw the necessary and logical consequences of his teaching for evangelism and world mission. Many would go on to become strong advocates for evangelism and cross-cultural missionary enterprises because of the insights they drew from his writings on free will.[76]

---

[74] For the most authoritative account of how Edwards's doctrine went on to effect subsequent generations, see Guelzo, *Edwards on the Will*.

[75] Robert Caldwell, *Theologies of the American Revivalists: From Whitefield to Finney* (Downer's Grove, IL: IVP Academic, 2017), 99. Italics original.

[76] For example, Nathaniel Emmons would go on to be one of the founders and the first president of the Massachusetts Missionary Society. He would also be a key player in the formation of Andover Theological seminary (a hotbed for missionary activity in the late 18th and early 19th century). Also, Samuel Hopkins established a school for Negro missions to Africa.

CHAPTER 4
THE VERBAL PROCLAMATION OF THE GOSPEL

THIS CHAPTER WILL SEEK TO PROVE the claim that Edwards's doctrine of the verbal proclamation of the gospel, the message that Jesus Christ came into the world to save sinners from eternal damnation, is the way in which the kingdom of Christ advances in the world. In other words, the proclamation of the gospel is the method of world mission. This proclamation can occur in a variety of forms, such as a sermon delivered by the preacher from the pulpit in the weekly gathering of believers. It could also be given on the street by a layperson to a stranger. It could be communicated in the context of a cross-cultural encounter and delivered through an interpreter. Thus, there are a variety of expressions that this method can take. Yet, the preaching of the gospel is the means by which this theology of mission is expressed and communicated to the world. Edwards shows in numerous places that the manner in which the gospel goes forth to the ends of the earth is by a verbal communication of the gospel.[1] If one is ignorant of the gospel, they will remain in their sins and be consigned to eternal

---

[1] The emphasis in this chapter is on the verbal proclamation of the gospel. As we will see in Edwards's scheme, the priority for gospel communication is via oral communication. We will assume that a written form of communication could also be communicated as well. A person could read the gospel in written form and come to saving faith in that manner. Yet, since Edwards's focus primarily on the verbal method, our priority will also concentrate on the method that involves speaking and listening. For an example of when Edwards refers to a communication of the gospel in written form, in his treatise, *An Humble Attempt,* Edwards recounts a story of the conversion of twenty thousand people living in Germany who were converted simply through reading the Bible in their own language. Edwards, *An Humble Attempt WJE* 5:363.

punishment in hell. In short, there is no salvation outside of the message of Jesus Christ being communicated to sinners.[2]

As per our prescribed strategy, our method of presentation will be to first present a historical-theological analysis of Edwards's doctrine. The second section of this chapter will present a missional reading of Edwards's representative work for this doctrine—*An Humble Attempt*. Again, the definition of mission necessarily involves any idea that might communicate the advancement of the Christian religion, especially into areas outside Christendom.

The Method of a Theology of Mission: A Historical-Theological Survey

In this section, we will show Edwards's doctrine of the verbal proclamation of the gospel as essential to the advancement of the Christian religion on earth in three points. First, his claim that the church's primary task is to preach the message is clear sign that Edwards saw the verbal preaching of the gospel as necessary for the advancement of the Christian religion on earth. Second, Edwards believed gospel preaching would be met with success. Therein, the kingdom of Christ on earth would advance in the world through the proclamation of the gospel message. Edwards's belief that the Bible prophesies that the ends of the earth will surely come to a saving knowledge of Jesus Christ. This end is a foregone conclusion because God has promised it. Edwards says that the only way this conversion happens is through a verbal communication of the gospel to the unbeliever. This doctrine ensures the success of world mission because it is guaranteed by God. Third, Edwards used typology for highlighting missional themes. More specifically, Edwards employs a creative hermeneutical tool to show how the proclamation of the gospel to all nations is found in images within the narrative texts of Scripture. This point shows that Scripture not only commands the church to promulgate

---

[2]For Edwards, the verbal proclamation of the gospel does not ensure the salvation of the sinner. That person must respond positively to its message by repentance and faith. Embedded within that message, there is the assumption that the sinner will know how to appropriately respond. If some information about the person and work of Jesus Christ is communicated, with no instructions on how to get in on its saving benefits, that information is ultimately useless for their plight. And quite obviously, if the listener rejects the content and responds negatively to its message, that person will receive not the benefits, but the judgments communicated in that message. In this paper, we will assume that whenever Edwards speaks of the gospel being communicated or proclaimed, the proper directives for the benefits and judgments are explicit (or implicit) within.

the gospel through its direct imperatives and prophetic utterances, but it also does so through the use of typology. The Bible demonstrates the verbal proclamation of the gospel as essential to world mission through its types and shadows as well. These three areas taken together provide a convincing argument that, for Edwards, the means by which the kingdom of Christ is advanced in the world is through a verbal proclamation of the gospel.

For Edwards, the conversion of the non-Christian does not happen outside of the verbal proclamation of the gospel because it is the only means by which someone is saved.[3] There have been debates between scholars concerning Edwards's position on the salvation of those whom have never heard the gospel message.[4] They have sought to answer the question: did Edwards believe that a moral person who has never heard the gospel of Jesus Christ be saved? While this is an important question, it is not the main focus of our analysis because all scholars would agree that world mission was important for Edwards. The point of debate centers on his private writings where Edwards would often work out theological conclusions. When reading Edwards's personal writings, one must interpret them cautiously because they are notebooks where he would try to creatively think things through. The theological conclusions he arrives at there are not really conclusions at all (provided they are not confirmed in his public addresses or otherwise stated in the text itself). They are unformed writings that are not meant to be complete and definite thoughts, meant for public consumption. However, even if Edwards held out the hope of salvation for those persons

---

[3] Edwards leaves no room for salvation outside of Christ. He says, "There is nothing appears in the reason and nature of things ... that can justly lead us to determine that God will certainly reveal Christ and give the necessary means of grace, or ... saving grace, and so eternal salvation, to those heathen that are sincere." Even if the heathen conforms to Christian standards of morality and proves to be a sincere person, that fact does not take away their sin and guilt. They still stand condemned before a holy god. Edwards, *The "Miscellanies": (Entry Nos. 1153–1360)*, *WJE* 23:56.

[4] On the one side are scholars like Anri Morimoto and Gerald McDermott. They have held the view that while Edwards did not explicitly embrace a doctrine of inclusivism, Edwards's private writings reveal a different story. Morimoto says that Edwards's private writings articulate that those ignorant of the gospel will be saved in the end. McDermott's position is not as forceful. He says that Edwards's private writings put the reader on a trajectory towards inclusivism. In other words, Edwards did not explicit articulate a universal salvation, but one can easily (if not necessarily) be led to that conclusion if his arguments are played out to their logical conclusions. On the other side is Greg D. Gilbert. He rejects these claims by saying Edwards's public and private writings hold not hope of salvation for those outside Christ. Greg D. Gilbert, "The Nations Will Worship: Jonathan Edwards and the Salvation of the Heathen," *TRINJ* 23 (2002): 53; Anri Morimoto, *Jonathan Edwards and the Catholic Vision of Salvation* (Univeristy Park, PA: Pennsylvania State Publishing, 1995); Gerald McDermott, *Jonathan Edwards Confronts the Gods*.

who have never heard the message, the church is nevertheless called to verbally communicate that message of salvation. The church, especially its ministers, have an obligation to preach the gospel to the non-Christian. In both his public and private writings, Edwards clearly expressed a vision of God's glory covering the earth—and the conversion of the individual is the essential substance of that scheme. People from all the nations would experience God's saving mercies.[5] In short, Edwards called for those who are outside of the saving knowledge of Jesus Christ to repent of their sins and turn to Jesus Christ for salvation. Central to the claim in this chapter is that Edwards's call to preach the gospel had a particular emphasis for those outside Christendom.

The Call to Preach the Gospel

Undoubtedly, Edwards was an advocate for evangelism and mission. His publishing of David Brainerd's personal writings, his work among the Native American tribes of western Massachusetts, and his involvement in the colonial awakenings are well-known. His preaching and promotion for the spread of the Christian religion is clear throughout nearly every account of Edwards's life and teaching. The claim here, in this present research, is more specific. Our argument is that Edwards developed his doctrine of the verbal proclamation of the gospel with a distinctly missional emphasis. In other words, when one reads his evangelistic sermons and treatises, Edwards places its trajectory to the Gentile nations. The course of the gospel is to arrive and reach out to all peoples of the earth. Since non-Christian nations are included in God's saving purposes, the goal of the verbal proclamation of the gospel is to reach these places. In short, Edwards believed that the kingdom of Christ on earth would advance through a verbal communication of the gospel into non-Christian lands.

This task began with a call for the church to preach the gospel. This mandate finds its grounding in Christ's mission. Jesus came to be the "light

---

[5] This statement does not mean that everyone will be saved. Anyone with even the slightest familiarity with Jonathan Edwards knows that he held a place in his theology for eternal conscious torment in hell. One of Edwards's main points in that famous sermon–"Sinners in the Hands of an Angry God"–is to show that hell is eternal. To show one example of many in that sermon, Edwards writes, "'Tis everlasting wrath. It would be dreadful to suffer this fierceness and wrath of almighty God one moment; but you must suffer it to all eternity: there will be no end to this exquisite horrible misery." Jonathan Edwards, *Sermons and Discourses: 1739–1742*, ed. Harry S. Stout and Nathan O. Hatch, vol. 22 of *The Works of Jonathan Edwards* [WJE] (New Haven: Yale University Press, 2003), 415. Italics original.

of the world" and "a light to lighten the Gentiles."[6] Since Jesus' mission was to "teach the nations," he sent forth his Holy Spirit to empower his disciples to go and do likewise. The task of gospel proclamation is a responsibility of the contemporary church, but especially its ministers. "Those ministers that faithfully preach the gospel of Christ are accepted of God, and are as a sweet savor to him, whether they are successful or no ... The preaching of the gospel is the principal means of glorifying Christ."[7] While the outcome of their preaching may or may not be immediately effective in bringing someone to saving faith in Christ, the minister's faithfulness to carry out the task brings great honor and glory to God.[8] But this is not only the job of the Christian minister. It is the duty of all believers.[9] After quoting John 13:34 and other similar passages, he says that the way in which Christians love others most supremely is by a peaching of the gospel. The "great errand" that Christ gave the world was to "'go and preach the gospel' ... on which they were to be sent after his resurrection, when he said to them, 'Go ye into all the world, and preach the gospel to every creature'."[10] Edwards calls on all believers to participate in this call to reach the nations.[11]

---

[6] *Jonathan Edwards, Sermons and Discourses: 1734–1738*, ed. M. X. Lesser, vol. 19 of *The Works of Jonathan Edwards* [WJE] (New Haven: Yale University Press, 2001), 714.

[7] Edwards, *Sermons and Discourses: 1739–1742*, WJE 22:206.

[8] The point here is that every time the gospel is preached, it does not ensure that a person will automatically become a Christian. In fact, the gospel might be met with a person accepting to rejecting its message. The result is entirely up to God. As we will see in a later section, Edwards does believe that the preaching of the gospel will ultimately be successful because, according to the promises of God, some persons will inevitably respond positively to its preaching.

[9] Edwards, *Sermons and Discourses: 1743–1758*, WJE 25:334.

[10] Ibid., 335.

[11] Surprisingly, when reading Edwards, one does not often encounter direct commands for his audience to go and personally evangelize others. There are no strategies given as to how one might persuade someone to come to faith in Christ. Even less do we see Edwards calling for individuals to preach the gospel to those outside Christendom. In the final chapter of this study we will see the clearest admonition Edwards gives to his audience that it is their personal responsibility to preach the gospel. That admonition is found in Edwards's sermon "The Things that Belong to True Religion." However, there is an overwhelming theme in Edwards's sermons and writings that the gospel will go forth to the nations. His treatise *An Humble Attempt* is a transcontinental call for prayer, that the gospel would go forth to reach the non-Christian nations. This begs the question: How will that happen? From the writings of Edwards, one clearly sees a narrative of the kingdom of Christ advancing in the world through spiritual means—not through carnal means. This point will become clearer in our analysis in the next chapter as we argue that the gospel of Jesus Christ and his kingdom on earth advances through a conversion of the heart. Therefore, while there are not often explicit commands in Edwards's sermons or direct imperatives in his treatises for the everyday believer to go and preach the gospel (though those do exist), we may infer from his writings that the command is present.

Again, throughout Edwards's sermons and writings on revival and evangelism, he places the takes of gospel proclamation on a trajectory to the non-Christian nations. At Pentecost, people from all nations were filled with the Holy Spirit and "divine revelation was sent forth into other nations besides the Jews."[12] Then, disciples of Jesus went forth to preach the gospel to the non-Christian nations. Formerly, they were in darkness, but a great light shone upon them. It allowed them to throw off their idolatry and ungodliness. "When revelation was sent forth out of Zion unto the heathen world, the light of it proved irresistible."[13]

The command to preach of the gospel will ultimately be met with success. As we have just seen, that success may not be in an immediate sense of a particular person's conversion. In other words, the preacher is not automatically assured that preaching the gospel will be met with someone coming to faith in Christ. However, Edwards envisions a future day in which the nations will come to saving knowledge of Christ. "Christ's aim to assert his right over mankind ... by actually bringing all nations into his kingdom ... will be accomplished."[14] Edwards continues by saying the nations will be a reward for Christ's humiliation as promised in Philippians 2:9–10. The reward of the nations as a gift to God will be acquired through "an universal conversion of the world to the Christian faith, and a bringing all into the visible kingdom of Christ."[15] This future day comes as a fulfillment of Old Testament prophecy (Isaiah 45:22–23 and Psalm 2:6–8). When the ends of the earth look to Jesus, they will be saved. The non-Christian will be given as an inheritance and the utmost parts of the earth will be received as a possession.

But before that success comes, the world will experience the judgment of God. Edwards sees a pattern in how God dispenses his grace. "This being the method God takes with the world, first to make a revelation of his dreadful majesty and justice before he reveals his grace."[16] Edwards says that this is how God acted in giving grace to the world through Jesus Christ. First, Moses gave the Law. Then, Jesus Christ came to save. The

---

This command is implicitly present in his visions of a future in which the Christian religion will go to all nations.

[12] Edwards, *Sermons and Discourses: 1734–1738, WJE* 19:714.

[13] Ibid.

[14] Edwards, *The "Blank Bible," WJE* 24:878.

[15] Ibid.

[16] Edwards, "Miscellanies no. 337" *WJE* 13:412

reason for this ordering was to prepare men to receive God's grace. In like manner, future events will happen in this order. "And so in the destruction of Jerusalem before the preaching the gospel to the Gentile world, and the dreadful destruction of Antichrist before the full revealing his grace to the whole world."[17] Edwards looks forward to a future day when the grace of God will be dispensed through the verbal proclamation of the gospel. But in order to prepare men for that reality, judgment must first come.

The Telos of World Mission

Edwards envisioned a future day in which the non-Christian nations would come to worship Jesus as king of the world. To be more specific, Edwards was a millenarian who believed the millennial kingdom of God would one day be established on earth. The Spirit of God would be poured out on all the nations of the world, ushering in the millennial reign of Christ. In that promised thousand-year reign of Christ, Satan's power would be greatly diminished and the success of the gospel would go forth with little impediment.[18] Missional ambitions would reach their climax. The Gentile nations would hear the gospel preached and many would believe. This future vision is not wishful thinking, but a certainty, guaranteed by promises from God.

There are a number of other issues one could focus on when talking about the telos of world mission. One categorical breakdown lists four consequences of this worldwide revival. Edwards anticipated "(1) convert the remaining Roman Catholics to the Reformed faith, (2) purify the church of Arminians, (3) bring about the engrafting of ethnic Hebrews into the one true Israel of God, the church, and (4) convert all pagans."[19] Each four of these aspects of Edwards's view of the future revival deserves special attention. However, for our purposes here, we will focus on the last point. Our definition of missions is especially about considering the advancement of the Christian religion beyond Christendom. One might even put a finer point on this definition by saying when speaking of world mission, special

---

[17] Ibid., 412.

[18] Other factors that do not directly relate to spiritual things will be changed for the better as well. External things like health and long life will be improved and expanded. Wars, famine, and pestilence will be eliminated. Economic prosperity of countries will drastically improve as they come to accept the Christian religion. Political relationships will be improved. Many such things will characterize the millennium.

[19] Michael Anthony Milton, "Millenarianism," in *The Jonathan Edwards Encyclopedia,* eds. Harry S. Stout, Kenneth P. Minkema, and Adriaan C. Neele (Grand Rapids, MI.: Eerdmans, 2017).

attention is to be given to the gospel's advancement into territories where Christian religion has not been traditionally present in some form or another. This much finer point would exclude the first three points and leave the fourth remaining and more prominent. Using that finer qualification is how this section of research will proceed.

Edwards's depiction of a future age of peace, prosperity, and gospel advancement was centered on the millennium. There are numerous places, mostly in his "Miscellanies," where he speaks of this thousand-year period. However, one of the first descriptions of the millennium includes mentions of its effects on non-Christian nations. He writes of the millennium,

> How happy will that state be, when neither divine nor human learning shall be confined and imprisoned within only two or three nations of Europe, but shall be diffused all over the world, and this lower world shall be all over covered with light, the various parts of it mutually enlightening each other; when the most barbarous nations shall become as bright and polite as England; when ignorant heathen lands shall be stocked with most profound divines and most learned philosophers.[20]

In this entry, Edwards speaks of the advancement of the Christian religion into areas outside of Christendom. He envisions a future day in which the non-Christian nations will be enlightened with the truth of the gospel. They come to know the truths of God and will make significant progress in all areas of life. Not simply limited to the nations or Europe, or the countries immediately connected to them, but also the entire earth. Edwards visualizes a time when formerly non-Christian nations will produce the most prodigious theologians. The entire world will benefit from the "new and wondrous discoveries from Terra Australis Incognita, admirable books of devotion, the most divine and angelic strains from among the Hottentots, and the press shall groan in wild Tartary."[21] The reversal of unbelieving ignorance to deep Christian devotion will surprise and bless the world. The global scope of this vision is unmistakable in Edwards's vision.

The Gentile nations will experience human flourishing in every sense. Yet, the pinnacle of human flourishing is the knowledge of Jesus Christ. This saving knowledge of Jesus Christ realized in the non-Christian nations will be the fulfillment of divine prophecy. Edwards writes, "That one great event

---

[20] Edwards, *The "Miscellanies": (Entry Nos. a-z, aa-zz, 1–500)*, WJE 13:212.

[21] Ibid., 212.

of the conversion of the Gentile world from idols to the acknowledgment and worship of the God of Israel ... is a great and glorious seal and evidence of the divine mission of Jesus of Nazareth, and of his true Messiahship."[22]

In each of these images of a future day, the question arises: How is this future day realized? Edwards is sure to say that it will not be through military might or political maneuvering. He says, "[God's] Spirit shall be gloriously poured out for the wonderful revival and propagation of religion. This great work shall be accomplished, not by the authority of princes, nor by the wisdom of learned men, but by God's Holy Spirit."[23] The gospel will not advance on the earth though carnal means. It will only make its progress through spiritual means. This point does not not rule out God's use of earthly means to make people ready to receive gospel truths. As we have seen, that method is an important way that God chooses to prepare the nations to hear the verbal proclamation of the gospel.[24] The way that it happens is through a preaching of the gospel. Edwards makes this point in no uncertain terms. Commenting on Revelation 14:6–8, he writes, "[Speak] of the whole earth's being filled with the knowledge and worship of the true God by the preaching of the gospel 'to every nation, and kindred, and tongue, and people,' as attending the downfall and dismal punishment of Babylon."[25] The whole earth is filled with God's glory because they are made knowledgeable of the gospel. How are they made knowledgeable of the gospel? They are made aware by verbal communication. In other words, it comes through preaching.

However, this point brings us back to the foundational doctrine that began our study of Edward's theology of mission—-the sovereignty of God. It is only by God's power that his kingdom might advance on earth. That way, only he will be able to take the glory for the accomplishment. Men will not be ultimately be able to take the credit for what God alone has done. Yet, the question remains: How will it be accomplished? The answer is given by Edwards.

> God, by pouring out his Holy Spirit, shall furnish men to be glorious instruments of carrying on his work; shall fill them with

---

[22] Edwards, *The "Miscellanies": (Entry Nos. 1153–1360), WJE* 23:303.

[23] Edwards, *A History of the Work of Redemption, WJE* 9:460.

[24] The idea that external forces like political and military power prepare the way for the kingdom of God to advance in the world will be examined in the next chapter.

[25] Edwards commentary on Revelation 14:6–8 is listed under his comments on Habakkuk 2:3–4. Edwards, *The "Blank Bible": Parts 1 & 2, WJE* 24:805.

> knowledge and wisdom and a fervent zeal for the promoting the kingdom of Christ and the salvation of souls and propagating the gospel in the world ... this great work of God shall be brought to pass by the preaching of the gospel, as it is represented in the fourteenth [chapter] of Revelation, sixth, seventh and eighth verses: that before Babylon falls the gospel will be powerfully preached and propagated in the world.[26]

That future day is realized through the verbal communication of the gospel. Edwards claims that it is only by the preaching of the gospel that the kingdom of Christ will be advanced in the world. Notice again that Edward uses the phrase "in the world" twice in this passage. The emphasis he wants to give to his audience is that the preaching of the gospel is to go out beyond the known world, into areas outside Christendom.[27]

Biblical Exegesis and Missional Typology

As we have seen, Edwards's exegesis reveals a missional awareness. He interpreted Scripture with an eye towards the global advancement of the Christian religion. Yet, one important subset of his exegesis deserves special attention—his typology.[28] Here, one sees Edwards as a creative theologian who tried to interpret Scripture in such a way as to bring imaginative connections to the text that are not immediately apparent from a straightforward reading of the text. In this interpretive process, concepts that are clearly found elsewhere in Scripture are brought forth to a verse, pericope, or

---

[26] Jonathan Edwards, *A History of the Work of Redemption*, WJE 9:460–1.

[27] Edwards certainly has a place for the revival or religion within Christendom. Immediately after this passage, he writes, "And there shall be a glorious pouring out of the Spirit with this clear and powerful preaching of the gospel, to make it successful for reviving those holy doctrines of religion that are now chiefly ridiculed in the world, and turning multitudes from heresy, and from popery, and from other false religion, and also for turning many from their vice and profaneness, and for bringing vast multitudes savingly home to Christ. The work of conversion shall go on in a wonderful manner, and spread more and more; more shall flow together to the goodness of the Lord and shall come, as it were, in flocks, one flock and multitude after another, continually flowing in, as in Is. 60:4–5." Here, Edwards envisions the non-Christian nations one day joining those who come from polite societies in worship. Ibid., 461.

[28] C.f. Janice Knight, "Typology," In *The Princeton Companion to Jonathan Edwards*, ed. Song Huyn Lee (Princeton, NJ: Princeton University Press, 2005), 190–209; Perry Miller, In *Images of Shadows of Divine Things* (New Haven: Yale University Press, 1948), 1–42; Stephen R. C. Nichols, "Typology," in *The Jonathan Edwards Encyclopedia*, eds. Harry S. Stout, Kenneth P. Minkema, and Adriaan C. Neele (Grand Rapids, MI: Eerdmans, 2017).

narrative that allows one to view from a different angle. Edwards uses this exegetical method in often fanciful and sometimes puzzling ways. Yet, he always does so with two primary convictions. The first is that Scripture is a unified story.[29] The second is that the Scripture is divinely inspired. Since these two convictions are closely related, one is able to stretch images and themes to cover a broad array of interpretive possibilities. For the purposes of our theses, we will show how he used this interpretive technique to reveal his doctrine of the verbal proclamation of the gospel. When these missional themes come out in his typology, we will call this type of interpretation a missional typology.

One example of Edwards's missional typology is his interpretation of the cock crowing three times, which is the moment Peter's denials of Jesus were made final and complete. He says that this passage can also be interpreted as a symbol of sinners being stirred to repentance.

> The awaking and crowing of the cock, to wake men out of sleep and to introduce the day, seems to signify the introducing the glorious day of the church by ministers preaching the Gospel. Many shall be awakened and roused to preach the Gospel with extraordinary fervency, to cry aloud and lift up their voices like trumpets. Peter's being awakened out of that deep sleep he had fallen into, and brought to repentance by the crowing of the cock at break of day, signifies the awakening of Christ's church that is built upon Peter; the rousing of the wise virgins out of that dull slumbering and backsliding state, in many respects denying their Lord, and bringing them to repentance by the preaching of the Gospel, to introduce the morning of the glorious times.[30]

When Peter hears the cock crow, he is brought to an immediate realization of his sin. He is awoken from a state of ignorance and instantly brought to repentance. In a similar way, men will be brought out of ignorance upon hearing the gospel preached. They will be awakened as it were from their spiritual sleep. This awakening will be like the dawning of a new day for the church. Edwards also draws comparisons to the parable of the wise and foolish virgins. When there is the cry at midnight of the bridegrooms

---

[29] That Edwards viewed Scripture as a unified whole is the central thesis of Stephen R. C. Nichols's book. See Stephen R. C. Nichols, *Jonathan Edwards's Bible: The Relationship of the Old and New Testaments* (Eugene, OR: Pickwick Publications, 2013).

[30] Edwards, *Typological Writings*, WJE 11:92–93.

impending arrival, the virgins are awakened from their slumber. They were also immediately brought to repentance upon hearing the call. Edwards interprets the church's verbal proclamation of the gospel as a similar call for the sleeping world to awaken from its slumber. They are no longer to be ignorant of God's plan of salvation. Upon hearing the gospel proclaimed, they are to repent of their sins and believe in Christ for salvation.

Edwards puts forth this type of missional typology in numerous places. For another example, one can see how he interprets the clean animals and unclean animals being taken into the ark. This scene is a picture of how God takes in both Jews and Gentiles in one people.

> The gathering of all kinds of creatures to the ark, clean and unclean, tame and wild, gentle and rapacious, innocent and venomous ... and the door of the ark standing open to 'em, and their all dwelling there peaceably together under one head, even Noah, who kindly received them and took care of them ... and to whom they tamely submitted, is a lively representation of what is often foretold concerning the Messiah's days, when it is foretold that not only the Jews should be saved but unclean Gentile nations, when the gates of God's church should be open to all sorts of people (Is. 60:11 with the context). When proclamation should be made to everyone to come freely (Is. 55:1–9), and God would abundantly pardon the wicked and unrighteous (vv. 6–9), and would bring again even the captivity of Sodom and her daughters (Ezek. 16:53). And those nations should be gathered to God's church to be one holy society with Israel that were wont to be their most cruel and inveterate enemies.[31]

Edwards goes on to say that the most violent creatures could dwell safely under one roof with other meek and defenseless creatures. They could peacefully cohabit together under one head—Noah, who is a type of Christ. There is a proclamation for all types of creatures to enter the ark. They are called to come into the ark and be saved. This calling in is a type and symbol of the church's gospel proclamation for all to come and be a part of God's people. This explicitly includes an invitation to the Gentile nations to be saved. At one time, Jews and Gentiles were enemies in the same way that ferocious and gentile animals are set against each other. However, the gospel message calls for them all to be reconciled with one another. Upon

---

[31] Ibid., 223.

hearing the verbal call to enter into the ark and the church, enemies are made safe from danger.

Another example can be found in Edwards's interpretation of the opening scene of 1 Kings where Nathan tells Bathsheba of Adonijah's treason. He attempted to set himself up as king instead of Solomon. Bathsheba then goes to inform David of the usurpation. Nathan's counsel to Bathsheba is a precursor to David's installing Solomon as king. Edwards says that Nathan's counsel is a type of gospel preaching. "The counsel he gave her, was the occasion of the introduction of the blissful and glorious reign of Solomon ... So the prophecies represent the preaching of God's ministers as the means of introducing the glorious kingdom of the Messiah."[32] In other words, the gospel is preached and thereby the kingdom of God advances in the world. Immediately after this statement, Edwards uses Isaiah 62:6–7 and 52:7–8 as support of this interpretation. In the first passage, Edwards wants the reader to see the watchmen as never ceasing to speak. As a result, Jerusalem will be made a "praise in the earth." In the second passage, those who proclaim the good news are lauded for their service by the watchmen of the city. Both of these passages speak of types of gospel ministers who preach the gospel to the earth.[33] They verbally proclaim the message of salvation, and God's kingdom in the world advances.

Other examples of Edwards's missional typology abound. Again, in each passage, the aim is to find the verbal communication of the gospel, especially to those outside Christendom. In one passage, Edwards looks forward to a day when the nations will come to worship Jesus as the true king of the world. Edwards makes numerous typological references to this future day. We will mention only a few examples. Edwards interprets the sun, moon, and stars bowing down to Joseph as a picture of a future day in which the Gentile nations will bow down to Jesus as ruler of the universe.[34] In this analogy, Joseph is a foreshadowing of the future Messiah that the world will come to worship.

---

[32] Ibid., 278.

[33] One must note the global scope Edwards has in mind for the preaching of the gospel. Edwards's use of Isaiah 62:6–7 confirms this mentality when the phrase "a praise in the earth" is used. In other words, Edwards's sphere of gospel proclamation is not simply limited to civilized society. However, Edwards does list an order or progression of gospel proclamation. He says that salvation was first preached to Israel. Israel receives first priority. Then, the Gentile nations. "This earnest, incessant preaching of ministers shall be in the first place to the visible church of God, that is represented in the Old Testament both as the wife and mother of Christ. She is represented as his mother." Ibid., 278.

[34] Ibid., 229–30.

Moving along in the Old Testament narrative, Edwards interprets the bronze serpent serpent as missional.[35] Not only did the nation of Israel look to the image for salvation (from the poisonous bites), but the non-Christian nations did so as well. Edwards lists a variety of Scripture passages in connection with this story that emphasize the gospel's progress beyond the people of Israel. "I said, Behold me, behold me, to a nation that was not called by my name" (Isa 65:1). "Lift up a standard for the people. Behold, the Lord hath proclaimed to the end of the world" (Isa 62:10–11). "Behold, thy King cometh unto thee: he is just, and having salvation ... And he shall speak peace unto the heathen" (Zech 9:9–12). "There shall be a root of Jesse, which shall stand for an ensign of the people; to it shall the Gentiles seek" (Isa 11:10).[36] "Look to me, and be ye saved, all the ends of the earth" (Isa 45:22). These passages are used to connect the original image to missional themes. Edwards is showing that one might interpret the pericope in Numbers 21 to foreshadow the salvation that is in Christ being communicated to the nations. The people of God are to call the non-Christian nations to look upon Christ in order to be saved. Moreover, Edwards notes the verbal proclamation associated with this call to look upon the bronze serpent. He says, "We may well suppose that when the brazen serpent was lifted up in the wilderness, there was proclamation made by heralds to that vast congregation, calling upon them to look on that."[37] Thus, Edwards's reference is that the brazen serpent lifted on a pole is an picture and foreshadowing of Jesus Christ crucified. The heralds who called the people to look upon the brazen serpent are likened to evangelists and missionaries to proclaim the gospel message. If they would look upon Jesus (in repentance and faith), they would be saved. In the case of the brazen serpent, they are saved from physical death by poison. In the case of the crucified Christ, they are saved from the second death.

Edwards uses this missional typology in his interpretation of the conquest of the Midianites. "The work of Gideon in conquering the Midianites ... is celebrated as a great work of God's power (Judg 6:14 and 7:2,7). But this is but a mere type of Christ's conquering the world by the preaching of the gospel."[38] The victory over the non-Christian nations by Gideon is a type of victory that Christians will experience as they preach the gospel.

---

[35] Ibid., 240–241.

[36] Italics are reflected in Edwards's writing of the verse.

[37] Edwards, *Typological Writings*, WJE 11:240.

[38] Edwards, *The "Miscellanies": (Entry Nos. 1153–1360)*, WJE 23:112.

In each of these examples, Edwards envisions the Gentile nations being brought into the promises and plan of God. They are included in God's salvific purposes for the world. The means by which the nations are saved (and all the benefits that come therein) is through a verbal proclamation of the gospel. This communication of God's saving message is seen both in Scripture's explicit calls to preach the gospel but also implicitly in Scripture's types and images.

An Humble Attempt: A Missional Reading

In this section, we will provide a missional reading of one of Edwards's treatises. Again, our purpose in providing such a reading is to draw out themes that relate to world mission. In this chapter, we will show arguments and themes that support the claim that Edwards taught the verbal proclamation of the gospel is the method in which the gospel advances in the world. A careful reading of Edwards's treatise, *An Humble Attempt*, helps one understand his theology of mission especially as it relates to this method of kingdom advancement. In this treatise, Edwards advocated for "concerts" of prayer. These concerts were intended to be coordinated acts of transatlantic prayer. Ministers from across the Atlantic would synchronize schedules with one another and have their congregations fast and pray for a rekindling of the revival fires experienced in earlier days. Embedded in the lengthier title of the treatise, the purpose of the document is to promote prayer for the revival of religion and the advancement of Christ's kingdom on earth.[39] This purpose statement fits exactly into our definition of a theology of mission. The expressed reasoning Edwards gives for writing the is for the advancement of the Christian religion on earth. This advancement necessarily involves the progress of the Christian faith into non-Christian nations. What might not be so apparent is how the verbal articulation of the gospel plays into this argument. Is prayer the primary means by which the gospel is advances into the world? Or is it the verbal proclamation of the gospel? In short, a proper reading of this texts shows these two as operating in tandem to achieve that goal. As we will see from our analysis, prayer prompts the Christian minister to go preach. It is asking for God to work in the heart and mind of the Christian minister to go and proclaim the

---

[39]The full title of the treatise is *An Humble Attempt to Promote an Explicit Agreement and Visible Union of God's People thro' the World, in Extraordinary Prayer, for the Revival of Religion, and the Advancement of Christ's Kingdom on Earth, Pursuant to Scripture Promise and Prophecies concerning the Last Time.*

gospel message to the non-Christian. Also, it is asking God to prepare the non-Christian to positively receive that message.

The first major section of Edwards's treatise is a commentary and exposition of Zechariah 8:20–22.[40] This passage is a "a prophecy of a future glorious advancement of the church of God."[41] Edwards has in mind that Christians should come together in an agreement to pray for worldwide revival. Prayer is the catalyst for gospel renewal in the world. Although God can do as he pleases, the church can move God to act through their prayers. The entire treatise assumes that prayer will move God to act in the world. Our purpose in this section is to show that whenever Edwards speaks of the purpose or reason for prayer, he says that it is to fundamentally involve the progress of the Christian religion on the earth. Occasionally, he will even mention that the progress of the religion comes only through the preaching of the gospel to the non-Christian.[42]

In one place he says, "[God's] church should be very much in prayer for that glorious outpouring of the Spirit that is to be in the latter days."[43] Edwards uses phrases like "the glorious outpouring of the Spirit" nearly synonymously with other phrases like "the advancement of God's kingdom" and "a gradual progress of religion." Whenever Edwards writes on this idea of the Christian religion advancing in the world, he is quick to show that prayer is a catalyst for that growth. To put it another way, when Christians pray for Christ's kingdom to advance in the world, God tends to answer those prayers. For example, the revival of religion experienced at Pentecost was in direct response to people gathering together to pray. "The greatest effusion of the Spirit that ever yet has been ... which began in Jerusalem on the day of Pentecost, was in answer to extraordinary prayer."[44] For another example, Edwards recounts two times in the recent past when he saw the Christian religion make great advances, Edwards says, "God was pleased to do great things for us in both these instances, in answer to extraordinary

---

[40]"Thus saith fore the Lord, and to seek the Lord of Hosts: I will go also. Yea, many people and strong nations shall come to seek the Lord of Hosts in Jerusalem, and to pray before the Lord."

[41]Edwards, *Apocalyptic Writings*, WJE 5:312.

[42]This point is not to insinuate that the Christian religion can advance in the world through some other means. Edwards never makes that claim. The Christian religion makes its progress only through a preaching of the gospel. Edwards does not need to make this connection between progress and preaching every time.

[43]Edwards, *Apocalyptic Writings*, WJE 5:348.

[44]Ibid., 356.

prayer."⁴⁵ God's people prayed, and then God answered their prayers. These events were done for "the promised general revival and advancement of true religion."⁴⁶ The prayers of God's people worked to advance Christ's kingdom on earth. Therefore, the first thing we can note about prayer is that it spurs God to action.

The Worldwide Scope of Christ's Redeeming Work

For Edwards, prayer can provoke God into action. But where—-and to what extent—will he act? One recurring theme of Edwards's *An Humble Attempt* is his repeated references to the worldwide scope of Christ's saving purposes. In these references, Edwards says that the kingdom of Christ will eventually spread to the ends of the earth. The proclamation of the gospel will be so effective as to reach the furthest peoples outside of Christendom.

> It is natural and reasonable to suppose, that the whole world should finally be given to Christ ... who is originally the king of all nations, ... God the Father hath constituted his Son ... to be "the heir of the world," that he might in this kingdom have "the heathen for his inheritance, and the utmost ends of the earth for his possession."

Edwards envisions a future day in which the ends of the earth will come into his possession. This inclusion of entire world into the promises and plan of God necessarily entails the non-Christian nations. Although the non-Christian nations do not yet belong under the earthly reign of Christ, they will inevitably come under his rule. Edwards points to the book of Daniel as a prophesying of this global kingdom. He highlights the imagery of Daniel 2 to make this specific point. One powerful nation will conquer and succeed another until the most powerful kingdom of all arises to crush them all. The kingdom of Christ is depicted as a stone that is cut out of the mountain–without hands–which crushes the statue which represents the four major kingdoms of the world. The other kingdoms are smashed into pieces which then disintegrate into nothing. But the stone becomes a mountain "and fills the whole earth."⁴⁷ Similarly, in Daniel 7, Edwards interprets the

---

⁴⁵ Ibid., 362.

⁴⁶ Ibid., 360.

⁴⁷ Edwards directly quotes from Daniel 2:34–35. This phrase is used in italics in the Yale critical edition, which reflects the original manuscripts. Edwards's highlighting this phrase shows the

four beasts as earthly kingdoms. They are consumed, each by another, until the Son of Man comes to destroy the final beast. The Son of Man is then given "a dominion, and glory, and a kingdom, *that all people, nations and languages* should serve him."[48] Again, Edwards's point is to express the universality of this kingdom. All are to be included in God's earthly reign. Edwards notes that the fourth and final beast should "devour the whole earth," but it is conquered.[49] He says that this language is meant to show the Son of Man's superiority. Thus, he deserves to have rule and reign over the entire world. The language is means to show "greater emphasis and strength of the expressions ... to understand the universality here expressed in a much more extensive and absolute sense ... that scarcely any can be devised more strong, to signify an absolute universality of dominion over the inhabitants of the face of the earth."[50] In short, Edwards means to say that no language can be greater and more encompassing of Christ's kingdom on earth.

Edwards goes on to list a number of references that are meant to express the universality and worldwide scope of Christ's rule on earth. It is meant to extend to the ends of the earth. There is no place that it will not reach. Quite obviously, this includes the non-Christian nations. "The time is coming when the whole world of mankind shall be brought into the church of Christ; and not only a part ... but the fullness of both [Jews and Gentiles], the whole lump, all the nation of the Jews, and all the world of Gentiles."[51] Scripture prophesies that people from all nations will come to a saving knowledge of Jesus Christ. "The main fulfillment of those prophecies, that speak of the glorious advancement of Christ's kingdom on earth, is still to come."[52] Thus, the church can look forward to—-and participate in—the actualization of those prophecies being fulfilled.

Again, the kingdom of Christ is not meant to be confined to one people or ethic group. It is not just for the polite members of civilized society. It is for the "world of Gentiles" and non-Christian nations. "The whole

---

reader the global scope of this kingdom. The kingdom of God established on earth is the final goal of all worldly governance and rule. It is meant to cover the entire earth. Ibid., 331.

[48] Again, Edwards's use of italics here is original. He stresses the worldwide scope of Christ's kingdom on earth. All peoples of the earth are to be included under his reign.

[49] Edwards, *Apocalyptic Writings*, WJE 5:331.

[50] Ibid., 331.

[51] Ibid., 334.

[52] Ibid., 335.

heathen world should be enlightened and converted to the Christian faith, throughout all parts of Africa, Asia, America and Terra Australis, and be thoroughly settled in Christian faith and order, without any remainders of their old delusions and superstitions."[53] The old non-Christian practices and religions of the world will be thrown off in favor of true religion. Edwards gives a hint at how this might happen. He points to the case of some years ago when there was a revival of religion in Germany.

> [They] were determined to throw off popery, and embrace the reformed religion; yea, and to become so very zealous for the truth and gospel of Jesus Christ, as to be willing to suffer the loss of all things in the world, and actually to forsake their houses, lands, goods and relations, that they might enjoy the pure preaching of the gospel ... with great earnestness, and tears in their eyes, beseeching Protestant ministers to preach to them.[54]

Note here the method in which Edwards outlines is the primary vehicle for the advancement of the kingdom of Christ on earth—the verbal preaching of the gospel. The verbal proclamation of the gospel is seen as supreme, worthy of forsaking earthly pleasure to obtain it. They were able to endure hardships and persecution only to receive the true word preached to them. Therefore, one should not neglect the preaching of the gospel because it brings about the advancement of the Christian religion in the world. Edwards says one's highest aspirations in prayer should be that of the advancement of Christ's kingdom on earth. Edwards writes, "Christ teaches us that it becomes his disciples to seek this above all other things, and make it the first and the last in their prayers, and that every petition should be put up in a subordination to the advancement of God's kingdom and glory in the world."[55] Every prayer should, in some sense, be about the global fulfillment of advancement of the Christian religion. Edwards is clear on this point about worldwide expansion. Immediately preceding this quotation, Edwards lists Scripture references that speak of God's glory expanding to the ends of the earth. To sample but a few, God's glory is "openly to be manifested in the sight of the heathen" (Ps 98:2). The kingdom of Christ will be publically displayed throughout the whole world, causing "every knee to

---

[53] Ibid., 411.

[54] Ibid., 363.

[55] Ibid., 350.

bow, and every tongue to confess to him" (Rom 14:11). Christ shall be given "dominion, glory and a kingdom, that all people, nations and languages should serve him" (Dan 7:14).

The Means by Which God's Glory is Spread

Edwards clearly says the gospel will be spread to the ends of the earth. The kingdom of Christ will gradually expand to reach the non-Christian nations. But the question remains: How will this be accomplished? How might the kingdom of Christ be advanced? Edwards clarifies this point near the beginning of his treatise.

> From the representation made in the prophecy [of Zechariah 8:20–22], it appears rational to suppose, that it will be fulfilled something after this manner; first, that there shall be given much of a spirit of prayer to God's people, in many places, disposing them to come into an express agreement, unitedly to pray to God in an extraordinary manner, that he would appear for the help of his church, and in mercy to mankind, and pour out his Spirit, revive his work, and advance his spiritual kingdom in the world, as he has promised.[56]

Edwards says that Zechariah's prophecy gives a model and example of how the kingdom of God advances through a combination of prayer and preaching working tougher in tandem. The work of revival begins with corporate prayer. This praying will cause God to work in the life of the church. He will inspire and awaken men and women to great spiritual devotion and exercises. Edwards goes on to say that the calls to prayer will spread throughout the church and a revival of religion will occur. The church will grow in their commitment to God in worship. Non-believers will see this excitement and devotion and be drawn into it. Edwards envisions the scenario:

> And that this disposition to such prayer, and union in it, will gradually spread more and more, and increase to greater degrees ...that this being observed, will be the means of awakening others, making them sensible of the wants of their souls, and exciting in them a great concern for their spiritual and everlasting

[56]Ibid., 317.

The Verbal Proclamation of the Gospel

> good, and putting them upon earnestly crying to God for spiritual mercies, and disposing them to join with God's people in that extraordinary seeking and serving of God, which they shall see them engaged in; and that in this manner religion shall be propagated ... till whole nations be awakened, and there be at length an accession of many of the chief nations of the world to the church of God.[57]

Many other people and nations will see the extraordinary power of God working in the lives of his people. And they will want to get in on what God is doing. This method of verbally proclaiming the gospel is the manner in which God's kingdom will be advanced in the world. Many nations will come to the saving knowledge of Jesus Christ because they witnessed people overjoyed in the worship of God. This process began with coordinated prayer.

However, the question remains: How will these non-Christian nations come into Christ's kingdom? Edwards goes on to clarify that it advances through conscious faith in Christ that comes only by a verbal proclamation of the gospel. He does this through his continued exposition of Zechariah 8:21.

> The inhabitants of one city shall apply themselves to the inhabitants of another, saying, Let us go, etc. Those to whom the motion is made, shall comply with it; the proposal shall take with many, it shall be a prevailing, spreading thing; one shall follow another's example, one and another shall say, I will go also.[58]

The people of God call the non-Christian nations to worship with them. It is an invitation to join them in prayer to God. Notice the verbal proclamation present in the phrase "another shall say." There is an oral articulation of one to another.

Edwards makes this connection between the verbal proclamation and the advancement of the Christian religion at different points at other points throughout the treatise as well. In one place where Edwards is speaking of the expansion of the gospel in the world, he links this idea with the gospel preached, "The gospel is represented as 'preached unto them that dwell on

---

[57] Ibid., 317–8.
[58] Ibid., 318.

the earth, and to every nation, and tongue, and kindred, and people' (Rev. 14:6)."⁵⁹ All peoples of the earth will be included in the kingdom of God because the gospel will be preached to them—-and some will respond in faith and obedience.

Summary

For Edwards, the verbal proclamation of the gospel is the means by which the kingdom of Christ will reach the ends of the earth. This method is that point of Edwards's theology of mission touches down to everyday life and ministry where the church participates in the gospel's global expansion. The church, especially its ministers, is called to proclaim the gospel and trust God to advance his kingdom through their faithful work. While there are other things that can ready the gospel's reception or make a way for salvation to break through, it is only by the verbal proclamation of the gospel that can truly advance the kingdom of God. This point will become more evident when we analyze Edwards's doctrine of the conversion of the heart.

---

⁵⁹Ibid., 331.

Chapter 5

The Conversion of the Heart

In the last chapter, Edwards's doctrine of the verbal proclamation of the gospel was presented as the means by which the gospel is communicated to the world. This doctrine is how the Christian religion is properly spread to the ends of the earth. But how is it properly received? Edwards believed that true religion is advanced in the world through a conversion of the heart. This doctrine will show the nature of mission. What does it look like? What does true religion consist of? Instead of the Christian religion making its advance through political or military achievements, it makes its progress through individuals coming to saving faith in Jesus Christ. Moreover, that religion is not fundamentally one of outward performance and sacramental practices. It is not characterized by religious formality or gamesmanship. True religion is characterized by a fundamental change of the inner person. Edwards says that God is glorified in the communication of himself to the human heart.[1]

Our argument in this chapter is that Edwards's doctrine of the conversion of the heart was often cast in distinctly missional terms. We will see that his doctrine was intended for all people, not just his fellow colonial churchmen. While his primary argument in writings like *Religious Affections, Distinguishing Marks,* and *Some Thoughts* involves those who are simply nominal in their faith (those within Christendom), Edwards regularly intersects this teaching with cross-cultural mission (those outside Christendom). In other

---

[1] "So God glorifies himself towards the creatures also two ways: (1) by appearing to them, being manifested to their understandings; (2) in communicating himself to their hearts, and in their rejoicing and delighting in, and enjoying the manifestations which he makes of himself." Edwards, "Miscellanies 448" *WJE* 13:495.

words, he will connect his doctrine of the conversion of the heart with the advancement of the Christian religion into non-Christian lands.

Our analysis will begin with a historical-theological study of the doctrine. We will seek to prove this present claim by showing how Edwards envisioned the communication of world mission. The first two points will begin by showing the methods Edwards rejected. First, Edwards believed that the Christian religion will not advance through political or military progress. Although he believed it was a sign of how God was moving in the world, he never equated it with the essence of true religion. Second, Edwards believed that the Christian religion will not advance through outward religious experiences or moral virtue alone. The kingdom of Christ on earth does not make its progress through religious experiences empty of religious affections.[2] Edwards outlined certain signs or marks that could be considered true and false versions of authentic spirituality. Our third point will present a positive and constructive case for how Edwards saw kingdom growth in the world. Here, we will show that Edwards saw the Christian religion advancing in the world by a divine act of God. He softens the sinner's heart, readying them for conversion. God's power then moves to bring them to repentance and faith in Christ. This divine act converts the sinner's heart, advancing the gospel in the world. Our analysis will then move to a missional reading of Edwards's key work in articulating this doctrine—the *Religious Affections*. This treatise will show how Edwards regarded true kingdom advancement into the world.

The Nature of a Theology of Mission: A Historical-Theological Survey

At the beginning of our analysis of the conversion of the heart, we might begin by asking the following question: what does Edwards mean by the heart? In other words, what is the nature of this inner transformation? What is to be effected in a conversion experience? In today's sense of the word, one might naturally associate the heart with emotions, feelings, sentiments, or passions. However, Edwards intends this term to be expansive, incorporating things normally associated with the spirit or soul. This includes but is not limited to things like the will, intellect, and understanding. In short, it is any

---

[2] Edwards says that the essence of the Christian faith consists in the heart being moved. He writes, "True religion, in great part, consists in holy affections." Edwards, *Religious Affections*, WJE 2:95. These affections are defined as, "The more vigorous and sensible exercises of the inclination and will of the soul." Ibid., 96.

faculty that allows one to reason, sense, feel, or think. In a sermon entitled "Saving Faith and Christian Obedience Arise from Godly Love," Edwards details the nature of what constitutes saving faith. He says in this sermon says saving faith is not made up of outward obedience alone. It is to be accompanied by a heart change. The inner man must be transformed. Saving faith fundamentally involves receiving God's grace in "the heart, or with the inclination and will of the soul."[3] Here, we see Edwards using the term heart interchangeably with the inward faculties that are associated with the decision making agency of a person. Conversion involves a transformation of the whole person. It involves a person's mind in their assent to doctrinal propositions. It also involves their heart—one's inner person being moved. "There is in saving faith a receiving the truth, not only with the assent of the mind but [with] the consent of the heart."[4] In his *Religious Affections*, Edwards defines the heart as that faculty "by which the soul does not merely perceive and view things, but is some way inclined with respect to the things it views or considers; either is inclined to 'em, or is discinclined, and averse from 'em."[5] Therefore, in our search for Edwards's doctrine of the conversion of the heart, we are looking to find a person accepting Christ not by an indifferent observation of him, but an inward acceptance of the beauty of Christ.

Moreover, the whole person is affected by this inner change. The inner faculty which accepts Christ then moves, inspires, and animates the entire person to good deeds. We can see this point in how Edwards bookends his treatise *Religious Affections*. The first major point Edwards makes regarding the nature of saving faith is that the converted person is inclined towards Christ in the heart.[6] Further, the very last major point Edwards makes in his treatise is that the converted person is one who bears fruit in his or her life.[7] That is to say true Christians are motived in their love to God and

---

[3]Edwards, *Sermons and Discourses, 1743–1758*, WJE 25:510.

[4]Ibid.

[5]Edwards says that a person has two faculties: the mind and the heart. The first is that part of the person that observes and perceives things. The second is that which has a tendency like or dislike something. Edwards, *Religious Affections*, WJE 2:96.

[6]"Affections that are truly spiritual and gracious, do arise from those influences and operations on the heart, which are spiritual, supernatural and divine." Ibid., 197.

[7]"Gracious and holy affections have their exercise and fruit in Christian practice. I mean, they have that influence and power upon him who is the subject of 'em, that they cause that a practice, which is universally conformed to, and directed by Christian rules, should be the practice and business of his life." Ibid., 383.

they demonstrate that love by bearing good fruit in their lives. They make religion "the main business of their lives."[8]

Whereas the entire person is affected, the change must begin in the heart. At present, we will proceed to delineate what Edwards conceived of as true authentic conversion of the heart. In order to make this point clearly, we will begin with a negative approach. In other words, we will first say how the kingdom of God does not make its advance in the world before we say how it does. This approach will eliminate some misconceptions at the onset, paving the way for a helpful discussion later.

Not By Political, Military, or Financial Might . . .

For whatever value he placed in them, Edwards believed the Christian religion would make its progress not by military or political might. He writes, "[God's] Spirit shall be gloriously poured out for the wonderful revival and propagation of religion. This great work shall be accomplished, not by the authority of princes, nor by the wisdom of learned men, but by God's Holy Spirit."[9] The times of refreshing promised in the prophets would come about through the promulgation of Christian gospel. This point was made in contrast to false religions who did make their advance through military might and political power. Edwards notes the growth of Islam came in this way.

> Mahometanism was propagated by the power of the sword, by potent sultans, absolute tyrants and mighty armies. Christianity was propagated by the weakest of men, unarmed with anything but meekness, humility, love, miracles, clear evidence, a most virtuous, holy and amiable example, and the power and fervor of eminent virtue, joined with assured belief of the truth, with self-denial and suffering for truth and holiness. And by such weapons as these it was propagated against the power, authority, wealth and armor of the world.[10]

The Christian religion's progress in the world stands in sharp contrast to Islam. Whereas Islam made its advance through the political power of its Sultans and the military might of its armies, the Christian faith spread

---

[8] Ibid., 387.
[9] Edwards, *A History of the Work of Redemption*, WJE 9:460.
[10] Edwards, "Miscellanies 1334" WJE 23:331.

through humble and weak people armed only with the truth of the gospel. Islam spread through the power of the sword. Christianity spread through the conversion of the heart.[11]

This approach was modeled first and foremost by Jesus Christ. When his enemies tried to aggressively and violently advance their own interests against him, he displayed humility and love. He advanced his kingdom in the world

> Not [by] shedding others' blood; but with all-conquering patience and love, shedding his own. Indeed one of his disciples, that made a forward pretense to boldness for Christ, and confidently declared he would sooner die with Christ than deny him, began to lay about him with a sword: but Christ meekly rebukes him, and heals the wound he gives.[12]

When one of his disciples attempted to advance the kingdom of Christ by violence, Jesus would have none of it. He rebuked his disciple and miraculously remedied the injury. The task of world mission is not to be found in enacting violence on unbelievers.

Edwards gives another notable example to exemplify his overall point. This time, he says that the gospel does not advance through political power. He points to the rise of Constantine to the position of Roman Emperor. When he arose to power and promoted the Christian religion, Satan, the "God of the heathen world," was stripped of his power and influence in the Roman world.[13] And as a result, the gospel was able to go forth with little hindrance.[14] In short, Constantine's rise allowed for gospel growth.

---

[11] Gerald McDermott's chapter, "Islam: The Left Arm of Antichrist," offers an insightful analysis of Edwards's view of Islam. Here, McDermott notes in Edwards's writings the dichotomy between the two religion's method of advancing in the world. He writes, "Because it appealed to base human desires, Islam never encountered much opposition. Christianity, on the other hand, contended against "the strongest empire ever." But while the gospel triumphed by the power of meekness, Islam won conversions only by the power of the sword." Gerald R. McDermott, *Jonathan Edwards Confronts the Gods,* 169.

[12] Edwards, *Religious Affections,* WJE 2:351.

[13] Edwards, *Sermons and Discourses: 1734–1738,* WJE 19:716.

[14] In a sermon outlining the various meanings of Constantine's rise to power, Edwards seems to say Christendom is synonymous with the kingdom of Christ. However, he clarifies himself saying that it is only the conversion of the heart by the gospel message that the kingdom of Christ really advances. "We may gather from what has been said that 'tis the gospel, and that only, that has actually been the means to bring the world to the knowledge of the true God." Edwards, *A History of the Work of Redemption,* WJE 9:398.

To be clear, at no point does Edwards ever say that the gospel's advance is synonymous with Christendom's political progress. He interprets this event as allowing the gospel to flourish.

> This was the greatest change and revolution that ever happened in the world of mankind, when the greatest part of mankind were soon brought utterly to cast off their old darkness, old gods, and old religions ... Before it was a thing unknown for a nation to change their gods ... But now the greater part of all the nations of the known world were brought to cast off all their former gods. That multitude of gods that they worshipped was all forsaken. Thousands of 'em were cast away for the worship of the true God and Jesus Christ, the only Savior.[15]

Notice the gospel advances through the nation's worship. First the outward signs of Christianity advances, and in this case, it is the Roman empire under Constantine. Then, the true and inward signs of Christianity advances, the nation's worship. Again, we must emphasize: Edwards does not say that the kingdom of Christ advances *in* the progress of Christendom. In the case of Constantine, it happened as the result of political expansion.[16] The non-Christian nations threw off their false gods when they heard the gospel preached to them. The Roman Empire was then expanded into other non-Christian lands. The gospel then took root and was able to spread with little hindrance.

Edwards also envisioned the chastening and purification of Christendom in the world as it expanded into non-Christian lands. In contrast to the greatest "revolution that ever happened in the world of mankind," the darkest day dawned when Roman Catholicism rose to prominence.[17] That rise spoiled the successes of Christendom's achievements. However, there will be a day when the work of Antichrist—namely, the Pope—will be undone.[18]

---

[15] Ibid., 715–6.

[16] Edwards will clarify through other points that Christendom's expansion into non-Christian lands does not necessarily or automatically result in true Christian conversion. However, we may infer that Edwards's opinion here (and elsewhere) is that the opportunity for true Christian conversion is greatly increased with the expansion of Christendom.

[17] Edwards said the rise of Roman Catholicism was "the darkest and most dismal day that ever the Christian church saw, and probably the darkest that ever it will see." Edwards, *A History of the Work of Redemption*, 9:409.

[18] See Edwards's "Miscellanies" 523. In it he says that the powers of Islam and Roman Catholicism will be overthrown. The reason they were allowed to rise to power was so that when

Another example illustrates Edwards's view that the gospel does not make its progress through political or military might. When the fortress of Louisbourg on Cape Breton was captured by the British in 1745, Edwards interpreted this event as divine judgment on Roman Catholic forces.[19] Edwards saw this as a possible fulfillment of his call to prayer in *An Humble Attempt*.[20] God was preparing the world for the true gospel to go forth. Admittedly, Edwards's language can sometime blur the lines between the advance of Christendom (outward society of those who identify as Christians) with the kingdom of Christ (true inner Christian religion). Yet, for Edwards, the two are not synonymous.[21] One way Edwards makes this distinction clear is how he defines a true conversion experience.

However, military and political advancement do have a place in world mission. Edwards says that power (and wealth) should be used to advance the kingdom of Christ on earth.[22] He says that some laymen actually have more influence and power than ordained ministers of the gospel do. He said that some laymen have inclined to not be passionate about religion because it might bring shame to their reputation. They might be perceived as excessively zealous, causing them to be publically shamed. But Edwards says that they should be like David was before the ark in 2 Samuel 6. David held the most prestigious position in all of Israel, yet he led all the congregation in his passion before the Lord. He was mocked by Michal, but he inspired the entire congregation of Israel to worship. These ministers have the ability to advance the kingdom of Christ in the world if they would just be willing. Edwards lays out a blueprint for how that might happen. "Great things might be done for the advancement of the kingdom of Christ at this day, by those that have ability, by establishing funds for the support and propagation of religion; by supporting some that are eminently qualified with gifts and

---

Christ's kingdom comes on earth, it will be proven to be far superior to the mightiest kingdoms of the world.

[19] Sometimes this fortress is spelled "Louisburg." See Mark A. Noll, *America's God: From Jonathan Edwards to Abraham Lincoln* (New York: Oxford University Press, 2002), 78–9.

[20] Marsden, *Jonathan Edwards: A Life,* 336–7.

[21] We may infer why Edwards so closely relates the two because of how he views the purpose of Christendom within biblical prophecy. Since the Roman empire persecuted Christians and worshiped their idols very publicly, God made his response public. He judged the nations for their wickedness on a public scale. While it seemed like the Roman empire held supreme power, God publicly demonstrated to all the world his infinite superiority over them. Edwards, *A History of the Work of Redemption, WJE* 9:387–402

[22] Edwards, *The Great Awakening, WJE* 4:513–5.

grace, in preaching the Gospel."[23] What is one way that rich and powerful laypeople advance Christ's kingdom? Edwards responds by saying they should give of their resources to support those who do preach the gospel. While this point has much overlap with our last chapter, it is included in this section to highlight our main argument in this chapter. Although it does have a place within the broad scheme of Christian discipleship, financial power does not advance the kingdom of Christ on earth.[24]

In summary, we must note how Edwards sees the progress of political, military, and religious institutional progress as somewhat intertwined. Again, our point in this entire chapter is to show Edwards's belief that the kingdom of Christ only makes it true progress through an internal conversion of the heart. However, this point does not take away from the outward forces that can cultivate growth.[25] Edwards envisions them all alongside one another in successive (and progressive) growth. God does not give the world into the hands of the church instantaneously. This incremental progress takes place so that the church can maintain hope in the world. He does this in order to "quicken and enliven their endeavors to propagate religion and to advance the kingdom of Jesus." Edwards continues,

> It is a great encouragement to such endeavors, to think that such times are coming wherein Christianity shall prevail over all enemies; and it would be a great discouragement to the labors of nations or pious magistrates and divines, to endeavor to advancing of Christ's kingdom, if they understood that it was not to be advanced. And indeed, the keeping alive such hopes in the church has a tendency to enliven all piety and religion in the general amongst God's people, that it should be carried on with greater earnestness and cheerfulness and faith.[26]

God allows the church to make progress in the world so that their hope can be kept alive. Without the hope of progress in the world, the church would be discouraged. However, as the church sees the advancement of the

---

[23] Ibid., 515.

[24] Whereas Edwards is using financial power in this example, the broader context of this passage make clear he is talking about all types of earthly power.

[25] Edwards says the opposite is also true. Non-Christian forces who fight against Christian nations can hinder and limit the growth of Christianity. Edwards points to the rise of the Roman emperor Julian and the restoration of ancient paganism. Edwards, *A History of the Work of Redemption*, WJE 9:406–7.

[26] Edwards, *The "Miscellanies": a-z, aa-zz, 1–500*, WJE 13:427.

Christian religion in the world, it will invigorate spiritual growth and bring about profound joy.

Nor By False Religious Experiences or Moral Virtue . . .

The second way the gospel is not properly received is by a false religious experience. This type of false religious experience takes an outward form of religiosity and an inward form of inauthentic spiritual encounters and practices. Our analysis will begin by looking at Edwards's view of outward religiosity and then his demarcation of false signs of conversion.

The first threat to gospel progress is that of outward religiosity. This threat is when people profess to be followers of Christ, but they are really just self-deluded because the inner man has not been changed. Edwards says that within Christendom, many people have not experienced true Christian conversion.

> To make a public profession of common, superficial religion at the same time that a man don't pretend to the internal, is in effect to make an open profession of being lukewarm, and so more hateful to Christ than a heathen. And who can believe that Christ, by his own institution, has appointed such a profession as this to be the terms of being received into his church and family and to his table as his friends and children?[27]

Making a public profession of faith in Christ that is not met with a conversion of the heart is not true religion. Outward religiosity is a false pretense in which the unregenerate try to convince themselves and others that they are truly accepted by God. Edwards's treatises *Distinguishing Marks* and *Religious Affections* are essentially written to combat this idea.[28] Simply identifying with Christ is not sufficient for salvation. According to Edwards, outward religiosity is also not a means by which the Christian religion advances in the world–because it is not true religion.

A similar idea to the aforementioned one is that of mere moral performance. For Edwards, the Christian religion does not advance through shows of public virtue. In a sermon entitled "All Natural Men Do Is Wrong," Edwards says that ethical performances are counted as worthless in God's

---

[27] Edwards, *Sermons and Discourses: 1743–1758*, WJE 25:360.

[28] The "negative signs" in both treatises serve to expose this idea that personal experiences are reliable evidences of saving faith when, in fact, they are not.

sight if not attended with faith in God. If a person acts with virtue that is absent of any desire to please God, that act is considered wrong.

> All that they do in an attendance on moral duties is done wrong: when they do acts of justice, and are honest in their duty; and when they are liberal to the poor, and the like ... But yet as they do it, as the act is performed by them, that act is wrong, for the reasons already mentioned, because done with a corrupt and rotten heart. And what is done is only a shadow without substance: there is the shell of the duty, but the inside is hollow.[29]

Men in their natural condition simply cannot please God. Their deeds must spring forth from a heart that desires to please God. The reason their deeds are considered wrong is because there is "no inward exercise of any internal grace, or virtue of righteousness, or charity in it. Nor is the end right. God, who ought to be the supreme end of all, is left out of the view and aim of the agent."[30] For Edwards, this is a negative way of saying that a conversion of the heart must come before deeds are pleasing to God. The way that does please him—and thereby advances the kingdom of Christ on earth—must begin with the inner man transformed by the saving grace of God.

Again, in order for deeds to be truly pleasing to God, they must spring from a heart that desires to please God. Yet, one common way that deceives a person into thinking that God is truly pleased with an action is by the religious performances. Edwards identified these false religious experiences in a sermon entitled "False Light and True." Edwards says that Satan often disguises himself as an angel of light and misleads people into thinking they are truly holy. However, it is not real holiness. These persons are self-deluded. Edwards writes, "There are counterfeit discoveries in imitation of those saving discoveries that are made of God, and Christ, and spiritual things in the work of conversion, that Satan himself may be the author of."[31] Edwards says that some people think they are converted when they are really not. Why is this the case? Edwards answers by saying these people do not really believe in their hearts. Satan is unable to produce anything like true conversion. "He can't let in divine light into the soul, nor anything

---

[29] Edwards, *Sermons and Discourses: 1734–1738, WJE* 19:527.

[30] Ibid., 527.

[31] Ibid.,127.

indeed like it."[32] True conversion produces a heart moved by "the excellency of the things of religion."[33]

...But By a Conversion of the Heart

Edwards believed that the Kingdom of Christ would advance not through political, military, or false religious experiences, but only through a conversion of the heart. The gospel would be sent forth into the world and it would be received by people in one of two ways. It would either be accepted or rejected. However, Edwards makes plain that the latter can be disguised. In other words, rejection can look like acceptance. This rejection can deceive others as well as the individual. This point is the explicit purpose of numerous treatises Edwards writes, most notably his *Faithful Narrative, Distinguishing Marks, Some Thoughts Concerning the Present Revival,* and *Religious Affections*. Edwards turns to reason and biblical history to delineate what are true and false signs of kingdom advancement. While there are many false signs of the gospel advancing in the world, one thing is certain: the kingdom of Christ makes its true progress only through an inward conversion of the heart. In other words, world mission takes place through individuals personally accepting the gospel message in their hearts. True religion is the reason Jesus Christ came into the world. Edwards writes that Jesus came to

> thence extend his blessed kingdom over all nations; not by outward force, but inward overcoming influence, by his Word and Spirit making them "his willing people in the day of his power" [Ps. 110:3]; and reigning in glorious light and holiness and love and peace forever: and the advancement of this universal and happy reign has been the earnest desire and prayer of the saints in all ages to the present day.[34]

Jesus came to bless the nations by converting hearts. He did not come to take over by outward force, but by inward influence. The advancement of his kingdom reign then becomes what the converted desire. Their hearts are affected and the kingdom of Christ on earth is thereby advanced.

---

[32]Ibid., 133.

[33]Ibid., 134.

[34]Edwards, *Apocalyptic Writings,* WJE 5:309.

Edwards believed that the Christian religion would advance in the world only by a conversion of the heart. This fact is evidenced in numerous places throughout his corpus. We will mention three examples here. First, in interpreting Isaiah 45:22–25, Edwards says, "This prophecy will have its last fulfillment at the day of judgment; but 'tis plain, that the thing most directly intended is the conversion of the gentile world to the Christian religion."[35] Edwards goes on to connect this verse's use of "confessing" or "swearing" with Romans 10:9.[36] Edwards highlights the act of believing in the heart as fundamental to true religion. Moreover, the belief in the heart is how "every knees shall bow, every tongue shall swear." Second, Edwards says in one of his "Miscellanies," that the first converts to Christianity from Judaism and other non-Christian religions were won by a preaching of the gospel. The "effect of turning them to Christianity" was not achieved by "by any natural influence of means."[37] Their conversion was achieved "by an extraordinary effusion of the Spirit of God, and a supernatural influence upon the minds of those that were turned, as is manifest from the extraordinary success [of] the gospel, and the swift progress it had against the greatest opposition and disadvantages."[38] The kingdom of Christ on earth progresses by converting the Gentiles (and Jews) through a supernatural impression on the mind. Here, Edwards uses that term synonymously with the heart. We know this because he goes on to say that they were converted by an impression of the "mighty power of the Spirit of God on their hearts, changing their very natures."[39] Third, one of Edwards's most extensive analyses of the conversion of the heart comes in his treatise *Original Sin,* part three, chapter two. This entire section is a lengthy explanation of how the doctrine of original sins finds application in redemption. His entire purpose in this

---

[35] Edwards quotes the passage as follows, "Look unto me, and be ye saved, all ye ends of the earth; for I am God, and there is none else: I have sworn by myself, the word is gone out of my mouth in righteousness, and shall not return, that unto me every knee shall bow, every tongue shall swear: truly shall one say, in the Lord have I righteousness and strength: even to him shall men come: ... In the Lord shall all the seed of Israel be justified and shall glory." Edwards, *Ecclesiastical Writings, WJE* 12:203.

[36] Edwards quotes the verse as follows, "If thou shalt confess with thy mouth the Lord Jesus, and shalt believe in thine heart, that God hath raised him from the dead, thou shalt be saved: for with the heart man believeth unto righteousness, and with the mouth confession is made unto salvation."

[37] Edwards, *The "Miscellanies": (Entry Nos. 501–832), WJE* 18:199.

[38] Ibid., 199.

[39] Ibid., 200.

chapter is to show how conversion is in its essence a "change of state."[40] He goes on to define what he means by this change of state. He says it is identical to Scripture's language of a "circumcision of the heart" and the Spirit giving a "new heart." Edwards then connects this language with world mission. He says that the gospel advances in the world only by a conversion of the heart.

> That it is a truth of the utmost certainty, with respect to every man, born of the race of Adam, by ordinary generation, that *unless he be born again, he cannot see the kingdom of God.* This is true, not only of the heathen, but of them that are born of the professing people of God, as Nicodemus, and the Jews, and every man born of the flesh.[41]

Edwards says that unless individuals experience a conversion of the heart, they will not be saved. This fact is true of every person, regardless of his or her race. Thus, Edwards casts his doctrine within the context of global mission. If a person is born outside of Christendom, they still must experience that inner change. The gospel makes its progress into non-Christian lands only by a conversion of the heart.

Immediate and Affective Knowledge

The conversion of the heart is a divine act. It is something only God can do, not something man can conjure up within himself. Additionally, it is not something that one person can impart to another person. Whereas gospel preachers are indispensable to the process of world missions, a person cannot immediately communicate salvation to another. Only God can immediately communicate salvation. This point is made clearly in one of Edwards's most famous sermons—*A Divine and Supernatural Light Immediately Imparted to the Soul by the Spirit of God*. As the subtitle of this sermon indicates, the "light" of conversion is imparted by Spirit of God (divine) in an immediate way (no mediator, directly from God). This light imparted by God to the soul is the only thing which saves a person.[42] Edwards writes, "This light,

---

[40] Edwards, *Original Sin*, WJE 3:361.

[41] Edwards, *Original Sin*, WJE 3:370. Italics original.

[42] Again, Edwards uses the term "soul" synonymously with the "heart." Whereas there might be some subtle distinction that has implications elsewhere, our purpose is to show that whenever the terms are used, they both communicate the idea of the inner person being entirely changed.

and this only, will bring the soul to a saving close with Christ. It conforms the heart to the gospel."[43]

Not only is true spiritual knowledge from God alone and immediately imparted to his elect, that knowledge is affective. Saving knowledge does not come merely through a simple ascent to doctrinal propositions.[44] It comes through a spiritual acceptation of that divine truth. Edwards saw an important nuance of the conversion experience, which led him to make a distinction between intellectual agreement to spiritual truth and a heartfelt accepting of that truth. Oliver Crisp writes, "For Edwards, true knowledge of a thing is affective knowledge ... there is a distinction to be made between knowledge by *description* and knowledge by *acquaintance* ... Without acquaintance, such knowledge is always notional; it is never affective."[45]

This point is made especially vivid in one of Edwards's most famous analogies. In this analogy, he likens intellectual and spiritual affectedness to the eating of honey. Edwards writes, "There is a difference between having a rational judgment that honey is sweet, and having a sense of its sweetness. A man may have the former, that knows not how honey tastes; but a man can't have the latter, unless he has an idea of the taste of honey in his mind."[46] A person is affected by honey in a completely different way when they taste its sweetness. Merely intellectual knowledge about honey does not give one a sense of it. Only when one experiences honey by tasting it do they have a full knowledge of it. Edwards goes on to make the connection to a person's faculties.

Therefore, for our purposes, they are used to communicate the same idea. We know this because immediately after Edwards speaks of the soul being changed, he speaks of the heart in the same exact way. In essence, they do the same thing: they change the nature of a person. "But this light, as it reaches the bottom of the heart, and changes the nature, so it will effectually dispose to an universal obedience. It shows God's worthiness to be obeyed and served. It draws forth the heart in a sincere love to God, which is the only principle of a true, gracious and universal obedience." Edwards, *Sermons and Discourses, 1730–1733, WJE* 17:424–5.

[43] Ibid., 424.

[44] Edwards calls this type of knowledge "notional." Two sermons explain this idea at length. The first is his sermon "A Spiritual Understanding of Divine Things Denied to the Unregenerate." Jonathan Edwards, *Sermons and Discourses, 1723–1729*, ed. Kenneth P. Minkema, vol. 14 of *The Works of Jonathan Edwards* [WJE] (New Haven: Yale University Press, 1996), 70–96; The second sermon is the aforementioned "A Divine and Supernatural Light." Edwards, *Sermons and Discourses, 1730–1733, WJE* 17:408–26.

[45] Oliver Crisp, *Jonathan Edwards Among the Theologians*, 152–3.

[46] Edwards, *Sermons and Discourses, 1730–1733, WJE* 17:414.

> There is a wide difference between mere speculative, rational judging anything to be excellent, and having a sense of its sweetness, and beauty. The former rests only in the head, speculation only is concerned in it; but the heart is concerned in the latter. When the heart is sensible of the beauty and amiableness of a thing, it necessarily feels pleasure in the apprehension.[47]

For Edwards, the heart is that faculty where one can truly experience something. It is a faculty that either accepts or rejects that thing which is perceives.

Once this point is made, Edwards connects his analogy to the conversion experience. He writes, "God is spoken of as giving the knowledge of Christ in conversion, as of what before was hidden and unseen, in that [place]."[48] It is in the heart where one must affected in order to experience genuine conversion. An intellectual discernment in the mind alone will not save a person. The perception of Jesus Christ must be accompanied with a heart that sees him as true, beautiful, and glorious.

Another way of describing this effectual knowledge is that of participation. Edwards conceived of conversion of the heart—and salvation in general—-as participating in the fullness of the divine life. Edwards described this kind experience as a receiving and reflecting of God's glory. The creature accepts God's beauty and glory and then it is returned back to God.

> In the creature's knowing, esteeming, loving, rejoicing in, and praising God, the glory of God is both exhibited and acknowledged; his fullness is received and returned. Here is both an *emanation* and *remanation*. The refulgence shines upon and into the creature, and is reflected back to the luminary. The beams of glory come from God, and are something of God, and are refunded back again to their original. So that the whole is *of* God, and *in* God, and *to* God; and God is the beginning, middle and end in this affair.[49]

Note the language of being affected in the heart. The creature loves, rejoices, and praises. This type of reaction is the substance (and evidence) of truly

---

[47] Ibid., 414.

[48] Ibid., 418.

[49] Edwards, *Ethical Writings, WJE* 8:531. This concept is unpacked in detail in Tan Seng-Kong, *Fullness Received and Returned: Trinity and Participation in Jonathan Edwards* (Minneapolis, MN: Fortress Press, 2014).

being affected in conversion. This experience is a type of partaking in God's fullness.

This participation is sometimes called *theosis*.[50] While there is much misunderstanding and controversy around this term, we do not mean it to become or to join in the divine *essence*. We mean it to participate in the nature or fellowship of God. In other words, the believer experiences the overflow of God's fellowship.[51] The important thing here for our purposes is how Edwards conceives of knowledge by acquaintance. Only Christians can really *know* God because true knowledge of God is to have relational fellowship with him. In one of his most famous sermons, Edwards offers an extensive analyses of the believer's experience of salvation.

> [The redeemed] have spiritual excellency and joy by a kind of participation of God.... They are made "partakers of the divine nature," or moral image of God (2 Pet. 1:4). They are holy by being made "partakers of God's holiness" (Heb. 12:10). The saints are beautiful and blessed by a communication of God's holiness and joy as the moon and planets are bright by the sun's light. The saint hath spiritual joy and pleasure by a kind of effusion of God on the soul. In these things the redeemed have communion with God; that is, they partake with him and of him.[52]

Participation in the fullness of God means to have one's heart affected with joy and excellency. God's fellowship is communicated to them and that participation makes them beautiful. This is all to say that to genuinely experience salvation is to be affected in the heart. For Edwards, a true conversion is not merely intellectual knowledge that is in the mind only. It

---

[50]For a helpful discussion on this topic, see Kyle Strobel, "Jonathan Edwards's Reformed Doctrine of Theosis," *Harvard Theological Review* 109, no. 3 (2016): 370–99.

[51]"Human persons are taken up into the life of God by participating in the divine fullness. This fullness is the overflow of God's life to the creature in Son and Spirit and is received and rebounded as the creature knows and loves God from within his self-knowing and self-loving. This is the only true knowledge of God because knowledge of God entails a participation in his self-knowledge. Furthermore, since God's knowledge is affectionate knowledge, all knowledge of God must also share in that affection." Oliver Crisp and Kyle Strobel, *Jonathan Edwards: An Introduction to His Thought* (Grand Rapids, MI: Eerdmans, 2018), 150.

[52]This sermon is entitled "God Glorified in Man's Dependence." Edwards, *Sermons and Discourses, 1730–1733, WJE* 17:208.

must be one that experiences "spiritual joy and pleasure of a kind of effusion of God on the soul."[53]

Edwards says that to have intellectual knowledge of spiritual things, but no participation—or inward heart change—is like the body without the soul. The person who has the body but no animating spirit is dead. Likewise, the person who has the proper information about the gospel, yet is not effected by it is spiritually dead. A person can even conform to all the moral and ethical principles of the Christian religion, but they remain unconverted. "All notional knowledge and outward virtue without this, is but the body without the spirit; 'tis the soul of all virtue and religious knowledge."[54] It is only in a person's heart being effected can conversion truly happen. Therefore, we may conclude that, for Edwards, the advancement of the Christian religion does not happen apart from a conversion of the heart.

Religious Affections: A Missional Reading

A missional reading of his treatise, *Religious Affections,* allows us to see how Edwards conceived of true religion advancing in the world. In short, he saw this by a conversion of the heart. Being affected in the heart is what true religion essentially is all about. Written in 1746, the fires of revival began to cool. Edwards sought to soberly analyze what made up a genuine religious experience. *Religious Affections* is the result. He directed his attention both at Old Lights who attempted the discredit the work of revival and New Light excesses.[55] Edwards took up a comprehensive and systematic analysis of Scripture in order to discover what it means to have an authentic religious experience that is pleasing to God.

Edwards writes that true religion's aim is to "reach the bottom of the heart, and affect and alter the very nature of the soul."[56] This inner change is what constitutes the beginning and substance of true religion is. Edwards goes on to elaborate on true religion.

> True religion is evermore a powerful thing; and the power of
> it appears, in the first place, in the inward exercises of it in the

---

[53] We may rightly interpret Edwards's use of the term "soul" as an all-encompassing term that includes both the mind and the heart.

[54] Edwards, *The "Miscellanies": (Entry Nos. 501–832)*, WJE 18:89.

[55] Marsden, *Jonathan Edwards: A Life,* 284–5.

[56] Edwards, *Religious Affections*, WJE 2:343.

heart, where is the principal and original seat of it. Hence true religion is called the power of godliness, in distinction from the external appearances of it, that are the form of it, "Having a form of godliness, but denying the power of it" (2 Tim. 3:5).[57]

Edwards begins his treatise here by making a distinction between outward and inward exercises. True religion is not found in the external forms of religion, however important those practices might be. The true power of religion is found in the heart. In this next section, we will continue to demonstrate how Edwards connected this point with world mission. The first thing we will see is Edward's observation that there is a threat to true religion spreading in the world.

The Threat to World Mission

Without the distinction between inward heart movements and outward exercises, Satan is able to smuggle false religion into true religion. This demonic bringing in of false religion is how the devil works against the kingdom of Christ expanding in the world. Edwards writes, "'Tis by the mixture of counterfeit religion with true, not discerned and distinguished, that the devil has had his greatest advantage against the cause and kingdom of Christ."[58] The distinction between true and false religion holds great importance for world mission because it guards against demonic attacks against true religion. Edwards says here that Satan's greatest strategy against the advancement of the gospel in the world is to confuse the two. He goes on to say that this strategy of confusion has worked well for Satan throughout church history. "'Tis plainly by this means, principally, that he has prevailed against all revivings of religion, that ever have been, since the first founding of the Christian church."[59] Edwards proceeds to chronicle Satan's attempts to distort and confuse the revival movements of God from the early church down to the colonial awakenings. As the gospel made successful advances in the world, Satan endeavored to destroy the work of Christ by pretending to be a part of it.

This demonic deception happens by infecting the true beginning and substance of world mission—the conversion experience. Satan accomplishes his deception by encouraging people to falsely believe themselves converted

[57] Ibid., 100.

[58] Ibid., 86.

[59] Ibid.

when they are not. They are reassured by false promises and signs. Therefore, they make no attempt to examine themselves because they believe themselves to be saved by God. Remaining in this condition is a dangerous state for a person because they will be condemned in the end. Edwards succinctly makes the point, "[Satan] deceives great multitudes about the state of their souls; making them think they are something, when they are nothing; and so eternally undoes 'em."[60]

Making the distinction clear is important to advancing true religion because there is another way Satan can distort true religion. Not only does Satan smuggle in false religion when the lines between the two are blurred, but he also pits faith and works against each other. He does this by stirring up false teachers to deceive people.

> There is a sort of men, who indeed abundantly cry down works, and cry up faith in opposition to works, and set up themselves very much as evangelical persons, in opposition to those that are of a legal spirit, and make a fair show of advancing Christ and the gospel, and the way of free grace; who are indeed some of the greatest enemies to the gospel way of free grace, and the most dangerous opposers of pure humble Christianity.[61]

These persons appear to be "advancing Christ and the gospel," but it is merely a "show." In other words, they appear to be engaged in world mission, but they are not really. They claim to be true Christians, but they are not really. The works that the false teacher decries is the show of outward religion. And the "true" religion, according to the false teacher, is merely an inward faith. This attitude gives rise to a false humility. Edwards says this type of spiritual pride is the worst pride of all.[62] False humility proves to be a

---

[60] Ibid., 88.

[61] Ibid., 318.

[62] Edwards says, "There is a pretended great humiliation, and being dead to the law, and emptied of self, which is one of the biggest and most elated things in the world. Some there are, who have made great profession of experience of a thorough work of the law on their own hearts, and of being brought fully off from works; whose conversation has savored most of a self-righteous spirit, of any that ever I had opportunity to observe. And some who think themselves quite emptied of themselves, and are confident that they are abased in the dust, are full as they can hold with the glory of their own humility, and lifted up to heaven with an high opinion of their abasement. Their humility is a swelling, self-conceited, confident, showy, noisy, assuming humility." Ibid., 319.

stumbling block to others coming to Christ because it prevents people from coming to the "gospel way of free grace."[63]

There are other ways the gospel can be prevented from advancing in the world. One hindrance to the advancement of the gospel is a bad strategy of gospel presentation. Edwards says that unbelieving persons who have spent their whole lives in a non-Christian culture cannot be expected to come to saving faith in Christ through the force of scholarly historical arguments. However right and accurate those arguments may be, those arguments may not be received well due to their inability to be properly understood. Edwards makes clear that the gospel is not just for educated persons who have the ability to properly discern academic arguments. The gospel message is for everyone.

> If men who have been brought up in heathenism, must wait for a clear and certain conviction of the truth of Christianity, till they have learning and acquaintance with the histories of politer nations, enough to see clearly the force of such kind of arguments; it will make the evidence of the gospel, to them, immensely cumbersome, and will render the propagation of the gospel among them, infinitely difficult.[64]

The gospel is able to advance into non-Christian lands with effectiveness because it is should be able to be comprehended with a certain degree of simplicity. Edwards reports that many Indians have expressed a desire to learn more about the Christian religion. He says how miserable their condition would be if it was expected that they learn complex arguments that might lead them to saving faith in Christ. For Edwards, the gospel message, at its most fundamental level, is a simple message that is to transform the inner man.

The Sum and Substance of True Religion

For Edwards, the sum and substance of true religion is to be found in the heart. This is the point of his first positive sign of authentic conversion. "Affections that are truly spiritual and gracious, do arise from those influences and operations on the heart, which are *spiritual, supernatural* and

---

[63] Ibid., 318.
[64] Ibid., 304.

divine."[65] This statement sets the tone for the rest of the treatise. All of the other points assume this one and are built on it. Edwards is saying that conversion happens in the heart. Authentic Christianity is about an inward transformation. Edwards argues that this is a work that only God can do.[66] Edwards's work can be considered a polemic in that he argues against several "signs" that one has experienced a genuine work of God.[67] For Edwards, not all inward movements of the heart are righteous and holy.

> There are false affections, and there are true. A man's having much affection, don't prove that he has any true religion: but if he has no affection, it proves that he has no true religion. The right way, is not to reject all affections, nor to approve all; but to distinguish between affections, approving some, and rejecting others; separating between the wheat and the chaff, the gold and the dross, the precious and the vile.[68]

Edwards's delineation between false religion and true religion is critical to understanding the nature of mission in the world. This explanation takes on a fuller meaning when one considers the context of Christendom where many had a false sense of security in their faith. Further, many arguments against revivals were being levied by fellow colonial ministers.[69]

---

[65] Ibid., 197. Italics original.

[66] Edwards says that this is the way that God works in the world. He acts so as to magnify his name and in such a way that man can not take credit. "'Tis God's manner, in the great works of his power and mercy which he works for his people, to order things so, as to make his hand visible, and his power conspicuous, and men's dependence on him most evident, that no flesh should glory in his presence, that God alone might be exalted and that the excellency of the power might be of God and not of man, and that Christ's power might be manifested in our weakness, and none might say mine own hand hath saved me." Ibid., 139.

[67] We can assume that because Edwards lays out "negative" signs, he is answering potential (or actual) objections to his thesis. Marsden says that Religious Affections was responding to two forces working against the authenticity of the awakening (and their emphasis on heart religion). First, Edwards sought to legitimize the revivals in light of their excesses. Second, Edwards defended the place of the affections over and against Charles Chauncey's argument to the contrary. Marsden, *Jonathan Edwards: A Life,* 284–6.

[68] Edwards, *Religious Affections, WJE* 2:121.

[69] These ministers were labeled "Old Lights," the most infamous being Charles Chauncey. They believed that the revivals brought dishonor to God because they supposedly disrupted the order of both church and society. Putting major emphasis on intellectual ascent to doctrines and their basis in rational thinking, these ministers held that there was no place for heightened emotions in the individual's religious experience. Edwards rejected this claim and placed affections as the seat of the religion. Chauncey in particular wanted to discredit the legitimacy of the revivals by pointing to its wild enthusiasm. He advocated a religion that could be rationally understood.

Yet, Edwards's purpose in writing this treatise was to help Christians know how to discern authentic religious experiences from false ones.[70]

In contrast to false religion, the picture of true religion is that the heart is affected. This picture is how the gospel will go to the ends of the earth. Edwards makes this connection in his twelfth and final sign of true religious experiences. In it, he notes a specific case of world mission in action. He comments on Philip sharing the gospel with the Ethiopian eunuch. Philip required that the Ethiopian eunuch be baptized as evidence that he "believed with all his heart."[71] Here, Edwards lays out the model for how cross-cultural evangelism should happen. The gospel is verbally proclaimed to the nations. They receive the saving message of Jesus Christ with a heart affected. Conversion happens when the inner person is transformed. Edwards says that this is an example for how the non-Christian nations are to be saved. He says, "[Converts] should profess that they rely only on Christ's righteousness and strength, and that they are devoted to him, as their only Lord and Saviour, and that they rejoice in him as their only righteousness and portion. It is foretold that all nations should be brought publicly to make this profession."[72] The only way that people are to be saved is by a heart devoted to Christ. They rejoice in their hearts. They rely only on Christ. Edwards points to Isaiah 45:22 in order to support his vision for world mission. The nations "ought to profess a willingness of heart to embrace religion with all its difficulties ... They ought to profess that all their hearts and souls."[73] Edwards makes repeated references to

---

"Chauncey argued that passions and affections had no legitimate place in the assessment of one's spiritual condition. Rather, he maintained that the sincerity of Christianity profession muse be determined on the basis of the temper of the mind, will, and actions." He believed while that one should pray for the outpouring of the Spirit of God on the nation, the current revivals were dominated by sensationalists who were during the church more harm that good. Nathan Parker, "Charles Chauncey (1705–1787)," in *The Jonathan Edwards Encyclopedia*, eds. Harry S. Stout, Kenneth P. Minkema, and Adriaan C. Neele (Grand Rapids, MI.: Eerdmans, 2017); See Marsden, *Jonathan Edwards: A Life*, 271.

[70] Edwards did not anticipate or want this treatise to serve as an infallible test for accurately determining individual's spiritual condition. In other words, he did not want someone to use his work as an impeccable tool for saying a particular person is saved or not. However, he did think it could be a useful guide for discerning the possible spiritual condition of a person. See Gerald R. McDermott, "Religious Affections," In *A Reader's Guide to the Major Writings of Jonathan Edwards*, ed. Nathan A. Finn and Jeremy M. Kimble (Wheaton, IL: Crossway, 2017), 95–110.

[71] Edwards, *Religious Affections*, WJE 2:414.

[72] Ibid., 414–5.

[73] Ibid., 415.

heart religion, emphasizing his position that the progress and advance of the gospel into non-Christian lands happens only though the conversion of the heart.

Summary

For Edwards, the verbal proclamation of the gospel is the means by which the kingdom of Christ will reach the ends of the earth. But that message must be met not only with the mind, but also with the heart. It is not enough to simple be aware of this information. Edwards calls that type of knowledge "notional." But it must also be positively received. This positive reception manifests in love towards God and joy in the things of religion. Edwards calls this type of reception "true religion" or "true knowledge of God." This conversion experience is the only way in which world mission can take place. It cannot happen through these political or military might. It cannot happen through false religious experiences. The kingdom of Christ on earth can only take place though a conversion of the heart. This aspect is the final aspect and the telos of Jonathan Edwards's theology of world mission.

Conclusion

This final chapter is intended summarize our research and see Edwards's entire theology of mission into a concise picture. This exercise will allow us to view his theology in a snapshot as well as bring together all five elements of his theology of mission into dialogue with one another. Moreover, it will synthesize all of our findings into a coherent whole.

A Review of Edwards's Theology of Mission

First, Edwards's theology of mission begins with a view of the sovereignty of God. This aspect proves to be the basis on which all the other doctrines we list are built upon. In other words, the sovereignty of God is the *foundation* for world mission. Fundamental to Edwards's doctrine is a trinitarian framework. Flowing out of an intra-Trinitarian love between the Father and the Son that is held together by the bond of the Holy Spirit, divine grace is communicated to the elect. God is the source and fountain of salvation, and he sovereignly dispenses that grace to whomever he will. Moreover, God acts in human history to actualize his plan of redemption. From the beginning to the end of creation, the plan of God is to bring about a global salvation. That is, the purpose and destiny of creation is that God would be glorified in the redemption of a people from every tongue, tribe, and nation.

Second, Edwards believes that while God is sovereign over all things, humanity is not. The sinfulness of humankind creates a universal *need* for world mission. Edwards's doctrine of the depravity of humankind stresses the universality of sin and its effects. Every person—-regardless of their background, race, ethnicity, or gender—-is born in sin and in need of God's forgiveness. God maintains his supreme priority in the redemption of the world is the vindication of his name among the nations. The world has profaned his name due to their idolatry and wickedness. They deserve the just penalty for their sin. God judges the nations and he also extends his saving hand of mercy. In spite of man's innate depravity, there still remains a hope for the world. Edwards's creative doctrine of the *prisca theologia* casts a hopeful optimism for the progress of the gospel into non-Christian nations.

Third, Edwards creates a distinction that allows for the *possibility* of world mission. This doctrine of the universal ability and inability of humankind holds the two aforementioned doctrines together while also creating a prospect for world mission. While humankind is completely free from any natural hindrance that might prevent them from faith in Christ, they are morally unwilling to place their faith in him. They willfully reject God and choose to rebel against him. This doctrine creates the possibility for conversion in that human beings have the all of the natural capacities to turn to Christ for salvation. They only need to turn their hearts away from sin and rely wholly on the grace of God for salvation. Throughout his articulation of his doctrine, Edwards draws implications for world mission.

Fourth, people must hear the gospel message proclaimed. The verbal proclamation of the gospel is the *method* of world mission. This proclamation is the church's primary task in the world. Moreover, this task of world mission is one that will be met with success. Scripture prophesies that the glory of the Lord will cover the earth as the waters cover the seas. Yet, the only way this ultimate end will be achieved is through a verbal proclamation of the gospel. Not only does Scripture's imperatives and prophecies make this clear, but also biblical typology does as well. Edwards creatively employed the use of typology to show how the gospel must be verbally proclaimed in the nations for the kingdom of Christ to advance in the world.

Fifth and finally, it is not enough to simply have a notional awareness of the gospel message. It is possible to hear the preaching of the gospel and not be transformed by it. One must necessarily experience a conversion of the heart. This is the essential *nature* of world mission. The kingdom of Christ does not advance on earth through political or military might. It also does not advance by false religious experiences or moral virtue alone. The only way that the gospel truly makes its progress in the world is by a conversion of the heart.

Summary

As we have seen throughout the writings of Edwards, these missional themes emerge in varying degrees. When the entire Edwardsian corpus is taken together, the five major themes are all clearly displayed and form a coherent theology of world mission.

BIBLIOGRAPHY

Barshinger, David. *Jonathan Edwards and the Psalms: A Redemptive Historical Vision of Scripture.* New York: Oxford University Press, 2014.

_____ "'The Only Rule of Our Faith and Practice': Jonathan Edwards' Interpretation of the Book of Isaiah As a Case Study of His Exegetical Boundaries." *JETS* 52:4 (2009) 811–29.

Barshinger, David and Douglas Sweeney, eds. *Jonathan Edwards and Scripture: Biblical Exegesis in British North America.* New York: Oxford, 2018.

Beaver, R. Pierce. "American Missionary Motivation before the Revolution." *Church History* 31 (1962): 216–26.

Berg, Johannes Van Den. *Constrained by Jesus' Love: An Inquiry into the Motives of the Missionary Awakening in Great Britain in the Period between 1698–1815.* Kampen, Netherlands: J. H. Kok, 1956.

Bombaro, John J. "Jonathan Edwards' Vision of Salvation." *Westminster Theological Journal* 65 (2003): 45–67.

Caldwell, Robert W., III. *Communion in the Spirit: The Holy Spirit as the Bond of Union in the Theology of Jonathan Edwards.* Studies in Evangelical History and Thought. Milton Keynes, UK: Paternoster, 2006.

Chun, Chris. *The Legacy of Jonathan Edwards in the Theology of Andrew Fuller.* Studies in the History of Christian Traditions. Boston: Brill, 2012.

Crisp, Oliver D. *Jonathan Edwards Among the Theologians.* Grand Rapids, MI: Eerdmans, 2015.

_____ "Jonathan Edwards and the Divine Nature." *Journal of Reformed Theology* 3 (2009): 175–201.

_____ "Jonathan Edwards on Divine Simplicity." *Religious Studies* 39 (2003): 23–41.

_____ "Jonathan Edwards' Panentheism." In *Jonathan Edwards as Contemporary: Essays in Honor of Sang Hyun Lee,* ed. Don Schweitzer, 107–126. New York: Peter Lang, 2010.

_____ *Jonathan Edwards on God and Creation.* New York: Oxford University Press, 2012.

Conforti, Joseph A. "Jonathan Edwards's Most Popular Work: 'The Life of David Brainerd' and Nineteenth-Century Evangelical Culture." *Church History* 54 (Jun 1985): 188–201.

_____ "David Brainerd and the Nineteenth Century Missionary Movement." *Journal of the Early Republic* 5 (1985): 309–32.

_____ *Jonathan Edwards, Religious Tradition & American Culture.* Chapel Hill, NC: University of North Carolina Press, 1995.

Davies, Ronald Edwin. "Prepare Ye the Way of the Lord: The Missiological Thought and Practice of Jonathan Edwards (1703–1758)." Ph.D. diss., Fuller Theological Seminary, 1989.

_____ *Jonathan Edwards and His Influence on the Development of the Missionary Movement from Britain.* Cambridge: Currents in World Christianity Project, 1996.

_____ "Jonathan Edwards (1703–1758): Eschatology and Mission." *A Heart for Mission: Five Pioneer Thinkers,* 79–96. Fearn, Scotland: Christian Focus, 2002.

_____ "Jonathan Edwards: Missionary Biographer, Theologian, Strategist, Administrator, Advocate–and Missionary." *International Bulletin of Missionary Research* 21 (1997): 60–7.

_____ "Jonathan Edwards, Theologian of the Missionary Awakening." *Evangel* 17 (1999): 1–8.

_____ *Jonathan Edwards: His Message and Impact.* Oswestry, UK: Quinta Press, 2003.

Edwards, Jonathan. *Freedom of the Will.* Edited by Paul Ramsey. Vol. 1 of *The Works of Jonathan Edwards* [WJE]. New Haven: Yale University Press, 1957.

_____ *Religious Affections.* Edited by John E. Smith. Vol. 2 of *The Works of Jonathan Edwards* [WJE]. New Haven: Yale University Press, 1959.

_____ *Original Sin.* Edited by Clyde A. Holbrook. Vol. 3 of *The Works of Jonathan Edwards* [WJE]. New Haven: Yale University Press, 1970.

_____ *The Great Awakening.* Edited by C. C. Goen. Vol. 4 of *The Works of Jonathan Edwards* [WJE]. New Haven: Yale University Press, 1972.

_____ *Apocalyptic Writings.* Edited by Stephen J. Stein. Vol. 5 of *The Works of Jonathan Edwards* [WJE]. New Haven: Yale University Press, 1977.

_____ *The Life of David Brainerd.* Edited by Norman Pettit. Vol. 7 of *The Works of Jonathan Edwards* [WJE]. New Haven: Yale University Press, 1984.

_____ *Ethical Writings.* Edited by Paul Ramsey. Vol. 8 of *The Works of Jonathan Edwards* [WJE]. New Haven: Yale University Press, 1989.

_____ *A History of the Work of Redemption.* Edited by John F. Wilson. Vol. 9 of *The Works of Jonathan Edwards* [WJE]. New Haven: Yale University Press, 1989.

_____ *Sermons and Discourses: 1720–1723.* Edited by Wilson H. Kimnach. Vol. 10 of *The Works of Jonathan Edwards* [WJE]. New Haven: Yale University Press, 1992.

_____ *Typological Writings.* Edited by Wallace E. Anderson. Vol. 11 of *The Works of Jonathan Edwards* [WJE]. New Haven: Yale University Press, 1993.

_____ *Ecclesiastical Writings.* Edited by David. D. Hall. Vol. 12 of *The Works of Jonathan Edwards* [WJE]. New Haven: Yale University Press, 1994.

_____ *The "Miscellanies": (Entry Nos. a-z, aa-zz, 1–500).* Edited by Thomas A. Schafter. Vol. 13 of *The Works of Jonathan Edwards* [WJE]. New Haven: Yale University Press, 1994.

_____ *Sermons and Discourses, 1723–1729,* ed. Kenneth P. Minkema. Vol. 14 of *The Works of Jonathan Edwards* [WJE]. New Haven: Yale University Press, 1996.

_____ *Notes on Scripture.* Edited by Stephen J. Stein. Vol. 15 of *The Works of Jonathan Edwards* [WJE]. New Haven: Yale University Press, 1998.

_____ *Letters and Personal Writings.* Edited by George S. Claghorn. Vol. 16 of *The Works of Jonathan Edwards* [WJE]. New Haven: Yale University Press, 1998.

_____ *Sermons and Discourses: 1730–1733.* Edited by Mark Valeri. Vol. 17 of *The Works of Jonathan Edwards* [WJE]. New Haven: Yale University Press, 1999.

_____ *The "Miscellanies": (Entry Nos. 501–832).* Edited by Ava Chamberlain. Vol. 18 of *The Works of Jonathan Edwards* [WJE]. New Haven: Yale University Press, 2000.

_____ *Sermons and Discourses: 1734–1738.* Edited by M. X. Lesser. Vol. 19 of *The Works of Jonathan Edwards* [WJE]. New Haven: Yale University Press, 2001.

_____ *The "Miscellanies": (Entry Nos. 833–1152).* Edited by Amy Plantinga Pauw. Vol. 20 of *The Works of Jonathan Edwards* [WJE]. New Haven: Yale University Press, 2000.

_____ *Writings on the Trinity, Grace, and Faith.* Edited by Sang Huyn Lee. Vol. 21 of *The Works of Jonathan Edwards* [WJE]. New Haven: Yale University Press, 2003.

_____ *Sermons and Discourses: 1739–1742.* Edited by Harry S. Stout and Nathan O. Hatch. Vol. 22 of *The Works of Jonathan Edwards* [WJE]. New Haven: Yale University Press, 2003.

_____ *The "Miscellanies": (Entry Nos. 1153–1360).* Edited by D. A. Sweeney & H. S. Stout. Vol. 23 of *The Works of Jonathan Edwards* [WJE]. New Haven: Yale University Press, 2004.

_____ *The "Blank Bible": Part 1 & Part 2.* Edited by Stephen J. Stein. Vol. 24 of *The Works of Jonathan Edwards* [WJE]. New Haven: Yale University Press, 2006.

_____ *Sermons and Discourses: 1743–1758.* Edited by Wilson H. Kimnach. Vol. 25 of *The Works of Jonathan Edwards* [WJE]. New Haven: Yale University Press, 2006.

Oliver Wendell Elsbree. *The Rise of the Missionary Spirit in America, 1790–1815.* Williamsport, PA: Williamsport Printing & Binding Co., 1928.

Fawcett, Arthur. *The Cambuslang Revival: The Scottish Evangelical Revival of the Eighteenth Century.* London: Banner of Truth Trust, 1971.

Finn, Nathan A. and Jeremy M. eds. Kimble. *A Reader's Guide to the Major Writings of Jonathan Edwards.* Wheaton, IL: Crossway, 2017.

Foster, John. "The Bicentenary of Jonathan Edwards' 'Humble Attempt'." *International Review of Missions* 37 (1948): 375–81.

Gibson, Jonathan. "Jonathan Edwards: A Missionary?" *Themelios* 36 (2011): 380–402.

Gilbert, Greg D. "The Nations Will Worship: Jonathan Edwards and the Salvation of the Heathen." *TRINJ* 23 (2002): 53–76.

Guelzo, Allen. *Edwards on the Will: A Century of American Theological Debate.* Middletown, CT: Wesleyan University Press, 1989.

Hart, D. G., Sean Michael Lucas and Stephen J. Nichols, eds. *The Legacy of Jonathan Edwards: American Religion and the Evangelical Tradition.* Grand Rapids: Baker, 2003.

Haykin, Michael A. G. "Advancing the Kingdom of Christ: Jonathan Edwards, The Missionary Theologian." *Banner of Truth* 482 (2003): 2–10.

Holifield, E. Brooks. "Edwards as Theologian." In *The Cambridge Companion to Jonathan Edwards,* ed. Stephen J. Stein, 144–61. New York: Cambridge University Press, 2007.

Hopkins, Philip. O. "Missions for the Glory of God: An Analysis of the Missionary Theology of John Piper." Ph.D. dissertation, Southeastern Baptist Theological Seminary, 2005.

Kane, J. Herbert. *A Concise History of the Christian World Mission: A Panoramic View of Missions from Pentecost to the Present.* Grand Rapids, MI: Baker, 1978.

Kimnach, Wilson H., ed. *Three Essays in Honor of the Publication of "The Life of David Brainerd."* New Haven: Winthrop Brainerd, 1985.

King, Jonathan. "Beauty." *The Jonathan Edwards Encyclopedia.* Eds. Harry S. Stout, Kenneth P. Minkema, and Adriaan C. Neele. Grand Rapids, MI.: Eerdmans, 2017.

Kling, David W. "Edwards in the Second Great Awakening: The New Divinity Contributions of Edward Dorr Griffin and Asahel Nettleton." In *After Jonathan Edwards: The Courses of New England Theology,* eds. Oliver D. Crisp and Douglas A. Sweeney, 130–41. New York: Oxford, 2012.

Kling, David W. and Douglas A. Sweeney, eds. *Jonathan Edwards at Home and Abroad: Historical Memories, Cultural Movements, Global Horizons.* Columbia: University of South Carolina Press, 2003.

Kellaway, William. *The New England Company, 1649–1776: Missionary Society to the American Indians.* London: Longmans, 1961.

Kuklick, Bruce. *A History of Philosophy in America 1720–2000.* New York, Oxford University Press, 2001.

MacCormac, Earl R. "Jonathan Edwards and Missions." In *Journal of the Presbyterian Historical Society* 39 (1961), 219–29.

Manor, James. "The Coming of Britain's Age of Empire and Protestant Mission Theology, 1750–1839." *Zeitschrift für Missionswissenschaft und Religionswissenschaft* 61 (1977): 38–54.

Marsden, George M. *Jonathan Edwards: A Life.* New Haven: Yale University Press, 2003.

_____ "Jonathan Edwards, the Missionary." *Journal of Presbyterian History* 81 (2003): 5–17.

McClymond, Michael J. "Hearing the Symphony: A Critique of Some Critics of Sang Lee's and Amy Pauw's Accounts of Jonathan Edwards's View of God." In *Jonathan Edwards as Contemporary: Essays in Honor of Sang Hyun Lee,* ed. Don Schweitzer, 67–92. New York: Peter Lang, 2010.

McClymond, Michael J., and Gerald R. McDermott. *The Theology of Jonathan Edwards.* New Haven: Yale University Press, 2012.

McDermott, Gerald R. *Jonathan Edwards Confronts the Gods: Christian Theology, Enlightenment Religion, and Non-Christian Faiths.* Religion in America. New York: Oxford University Press, 2000.

———. *One Holy and Happy Society: The Public Theology of Jonathan Edwards.* University Park, PA: The Pennsylvania State University Press, 1992.

Minkema, Kenneth P. "Personal Writings." In *The Cambridge Companion to Jonathan Edwards,* ed. Stephen J. Stein, 39–60. New York: Cambridge University Press, 2007.

Moore, Cynthia Marie. "'Rent and Ragged Relation(s)': Puritans, Indians, and the Management of Congregations in New England, 1647–1776." Ph.D. diss., State University of New York at Stony Brook, 1999.

Morimoto, Anri. "Salvation as Fulfillment of Being: The Soteriology of Jonathan Edwards and Its Implications for Christian Mission." *The Princeton Seminary Bulletin* 20 (1999): 13–23.

Muench, Marcus. "Consent." in *The Jonathan Edwards Encyclopedia.* Eds. Harry S. Stout, Kenneth P. Minkema, and Adriaan C. Neele. Grand Rapids, MI.: Eerdmans, 2017.

Pauw, Amy Plantinga. *The Supreme Harmony of All: The Trinitarian Theology of Jonathan Edwards.* Grand Rapids, MI: Eerdmans, 2002.

———. "'One Alone Cannot Be Excellent': Edwards on Divine Simplicity." In *Jonathan Edwards: Philosophical Theologian,* ed. Paul Helm and Oliver Crisp, 115–25. New York: Routledge, 2003.

Payne, Ernest A. "The Evangelical Revival and the Beginnings of the Modern Missionary Movement." *Congregational Quarterly* 21 (1943): 223–36.

———. *The Prayer Call of 1784.* London: Baptist Laymen's Missionary Movement, 1941.

Piper, John, and Justin Taylor. *A God-Entranced Vision of All Things. The Legacy of Jonathan Edwards.* Wheaton, IL: Crossway, 2004.

Rogers, Mark C. "A Missional Eschatology: Jonathan Edwards, Future prophecy, and the Spread of the Gospel." *Fides et Historia* 41 (2009): 23–46.

Stein, Stephen J., ed. *The Cambridge Companion to Jonathan Edwards.* New York: Cambridge University Press, 2007.

Stout, Harry S., Kenneth P. Minkema, and Adriaan C. Neele eds. *The Jonathan Edwards Encyclopedia.* Grand Rapids, MI.: Eerdmans, 2017.

Strange, Daniel. *Their Rock is Not Like Our Rock: A Theology of Religions.* Grand Rapids, MI: Zondervan, 2015.

Strobel, Kyle C. *Jonathan Edwards's Theology: A Reinterpretation.* T&T Clark Studies in Systematic Theology. London: T&T Clark, 2013.

———— "Theology in the Gaze of the Father: Retrieving Jonathan Edwards's Trinitarian Aesthetics." In *Advancing Trinitarian Theology Explorations in Constructive Dogmatics,* eds. Oliver D. Crisp and Fred Sanders, 147–170. Los Angeles Conference Series. Grand Rapids, MI: Zondervan, 2014.

Sweeney, Douglas A. *Edwards the Exegete: Biblical Interpretation and Anglo-Protestant Culture on the Edge of the Enlightenment.* New York: Oxford University Press, 2015.

———— "Jonathan Edwards, The Harmony of Scripture, and Canonical Exegesis." *Trinity Journal* 34 no. 2 (2013): 171–207.

Tan, Seng-Kong. *Fullness Received and Returned: Trinity and Participation in Jonathan Edwards.* Emerging Scholars. Minneapolis: Fortress Press, 2014.

———— "Trinitarian Action in the Incarnation." In *Jonathan Edwards as Contemporary: Essays in Honor of Sang Hyun Lee,* ed. Don Schweitzer, 127–50. New York: Peter Lang, 2010.

Todd, Obbie. "The Influence of Jonathan Edwards on the Missiology and Conversionism of Richard Furman." *Jonathan Edwards Studies* 7 (2017): 36–54.

Wheeler, Rachel. "'Friends to Your Souls': Jonathan Edwards' Indian Pastorate and the Doctrine of Original Sin." *Church History* 72 (2003): 736–65.

———— "Lessons from Stockbridge: Jonathan Edwards and the Stockbridge Indians," In *Jonathan Edwards at 300: Essays on the Tercentenary of his Birth,* eds. Harry S. Stout, Kenneth P. Minkema, and Caleb J. D. Maskell, 131–40. New York: University Press of America, 2005.

———— "Living upon Hope: Mahicans and Missionaries, 1730–1760." Ph.D. diss., Yale University, 1998.

Index

Below is a brief index of significant persons, places, doctrines, titles and topics.

Abrahamic covenant, 35
advance of gospel through worship, 122
Arminianism, 70, 72, 76, 80, 82, 84–89, 91, 101

baptism, 46
Bebbington, David, 79, 80
Brainerd, David, 98

Caldwell, Robert, 93
Calvinism, 73, 74
Cape Breton, 123
Carey, William, 6
Christ as second Adam, 64
Christian scholarship, 50
compatibilism, 92
concerts of prayer, 109, 115
conversion, 78, 80, 82, 85, 91, 97, 100, 113, 116–119, 121, 123–133, 136, 139, 142
Crisp, Oliver, 85, 86, 130

Davies, Ronald, 4
deism, 54
divine curse, 43

Edwards, Jonathan
    Distinguishing Marks of a Work of the Spirit of God, 117, 125, 127
    A Divine and Supernatural Light Immediately Imparted to the Soul by the Spirit of God, 129
    Faithful Narrative, 22, 127
    Freedom of the Will, 70, 78, 83, 86, 91
    God Glorified in Man's Dependence, 24, 72
    A History of the Work of Redemption, 4, 11, 29
    An Humble Attempt, 30, 96, 109, 111, 123
    Misrepresentations Corrected, and Truth Vindicated, 47
    Original Sin, 57, 60, 67, 77, 83, 128
    Religious Affections, 117–119, 125, 127, 133
    Some Thoughts Concerning the Present Revival of Religion, 117, 127
    The End for Which God Created the World, 4, 11, 23, 35, 42
    Treatise on Grace, 78, 80
    The Things that Belong to True Religion, 19
elect of God, 48
empty religious affections, 118
enjoyment of God, 39, 40
Enlightenment, 57, 72, 74
Erskine, John, 91, 92
eschatological hope, 33, 35, 49

eschatology, 7
evangelism, 92, 100
exegesis, 7, 104, 105

Fall, 45, 56
false religious experience, 125, 126, 142
federal headship of Adam, 64
foreknowledge of God, 89
free grace, 82, 93
free will, 60, 76, 81, 84, 86, 89, 92, 93
Fuller, Andrew, 6
Furman, Richar, 6

Garden of Eden, 43
Gibson, Jonathan, 4, 22
Gilbert, Greg, 1, 5
glory as God's creative purpose, 40, 41
grace of God, 49
Guelzo, Allen, 76
Guyse, John, 22

Hall, Richard, 72, 74
hamartiology, 45, 67
heart religion, 10, 91, 119–121, 124, 126, 127, 129, 131, 133, 134, 138, 139, 142
hell, 46, 96
holiness of God, 48
human agency, 87
human culture, 53
human dependence, 81, 83
human depravity, 9, 43, 44, 50, 58, 59, 66, 67, 73, 75, 126, 141, 142

imputation of sin, 43, 67
influence of laity, 123, 124
intellectual knowledge, 130, 133, 139
intertextuality, 48
intra-Trinitarian enjoyment, 39
intra-Trinitarian love, 25, 42, 141
Islam, 120

judgment of God, 48, 49, 100, 101, 142

Kimnach, Wilson, 19

libertarian freedom, 86
love as glory, 26

MacCormac, Earl, 5

Marsden, George, 29, 45
McClymond, Michael, 2, 5, 84
McDermott, Gerald, 1, 5, 6, 53, 84
merits of Christ, 65
military and political advancement, role of, 123, 124, 142
millennial reign, 49, 51
millennium, 52, 101, 102
missiology, 67
missional language, 16, 18, 24, 26, 28, 32, 35, 40, 42, 52, 78
missionary activity, 33, 63
moral inability, 60, 75, 77, 80, 89
Morimoto, Anri, 1, 5

Native Americans, 45, 59, 83, 98
natural ability, 9, 75, 77, 80, 83, 89
New Divinity, 93
New Lights, 133

Old Lights, 133

patterns of grace, 100
persecution, 113
Piper, John, 6
prayer, 110, 111, 114
prayer as dependence on God, 27
preparatory work, 56
prisca theologia, 45, 53, 56, 67
proclamation of gospel, 10, 15, 21, 41, 44, 95–101, 103, 104, 106, 108, 109, 111, 113–117, 138, 139, 142
progress of gospel, 1, 110, 111, 113, 115
purpose of creation, 36, 37

Reformed tradition, 71, 80, 83–85, 87–89, 101
revelation, 55
revival, 67, 100, 101, 103, 110, 111, 113, 114, 137
Rigney, Joe, 36
Rogers, Mark, 5
Roman Catholicism, 20, 101, 122, 123

simplicity of gospel, 136
soteriology, 7
sovereignty of God, 9, 23, 35, 43, 80, 81, 83, 85, 87–89, 103, 141
spiritual knowledge, 130

Stockbridge, 3, 20
Strobel, Kyle, 85
success of gospel, 27, 49, 51, 53, 64, 65, 92, 96, 99–101, 104, 134

Taylor, John, 57, 58
theology of mission, 2, 4, 5, 7–11, 13, 15, 20–23, 32, 33, 36–38, 42–44, 56, 67, 69, 95, 103, 109, 116, 141
Trinitarian communication, 25, 26, 39, 42
true and false religion, 134, 137

typology, 97, 104–109, 142

universal ability and inability, 9, 14, 67, 69, 70, 93, 142
universality of sin, 60, 141

Valeri, Mark, 71, 73

Watts, Isaac, 22
Westminster Shorter Catechism, 36
Wheeler, Rachel, 6, 59
wrath of God, 47

www.ingramcontent.com/pod-product-compliance
Lightning Source LLC
Chambersburg PA
CBHW071848230426
43671CB00012B/2105